ONLY ONE POINT OF THE COMPASS

ONLY ONE POINT OF THE COMPASS
Willa Cather in the Northeast

Marion Marsh Brown
and
Ruth Crone

ARCHER EDITIONS PRESS

ONLY ONE POINT OF THE COMPASS
Willa Cather in the Northeast

First Edition

Library of Congress Cataloging in Publication Data

Brown, Marion Marsh.
    Only one point of the compass.

    1.   Cather, Willa Sibert, 1873–1947—Homes and
haunts. 2.   Grand Manan Island, N.B.—Description
and travel. 3.   Novelists, American—20th century—
Biography. I.   Crone, Ruth, joint author. II.   Title.
PS3505.A87Z5849   813′.52 [B]   80-11384
ISBN 0-89097-017-3

Design by Wanda Hicks

The authors wish to acknowledge with gratitude permission to quote from Willa Cather, *Obscure Destinies*, 1930, Alfred A. Knopf and Willa Cather, *The Old Beauty*, 1948, Alfred A. Knopf.

Dedicated

to the innkeepers and caretakers
in the Northeast who helped provide
a proper climate for the flowering
of Willa Cather's art.

CHAPTER I

This *is* Grand Manan and this *was* Grand Manan—the small, isolated fishing island on which Willa Cather found a writing refuge in the early '20's. Now as then the fog billows in from the Bay of Fundy, over the treacherous hidden rocks that husband their dark record of fishing vessels bashed to bits and the lives of fishermen swallowed by the sea. It rolls over the circling weirs that decorate the coves. It surges inward, obscuring the grey docks decked with lobster traps; obliterating the contour of land, the silhouette of trees; engulfing the scattered, weather-beaten houses. It creeps, it fingers out, it settles in—until it has enveloped the island like cotton candy swirled about a stick.

The hoarse voice of the foghorn at Whistle Light breaks eerily into the stillness that has settled with the grey mist. It is the only sound. All else the fog has muffled into silence.

Gannet Rock Light, its vigil undaunted by the vagaries of weather, looms halo-like in the distance. It is the only point visible by land or by sea. All else the fog has erased. The world is enfolded in a great grey coverlet.

So it is that one feels as alone as if he were the only living creature on earth. To Willa Cather this feeling was gratifying. She enjoyed silence, solitude, and seclusion; to her the fog did not presage ill; it offered asylum.

But not always is Grand Manan fog-enshrouded and dour. There are the sunny days. Then the island sparkles. It glitters and shines. It beckons. It sings. Brilliance greets the awakening world on a morning of sun after fog. The waves, white-lace edged, never still, shoot silver sparks into the cobalt sky. The plump white breasts and serrated wing tips of gulls in flight catch the rays of the sun and pattern the blue with shafts of silver. In the distance the white sheen of a fishing boat separates the azure of sky and sea.

Not all, however, is silver and blue. The startling chartreuse of marsh grass fringing blue water explodes in the inlets. And trailing back and forth across the island flow the rainbow hues of a myriad of flowers both wild and tame: pink of wild roses, blue of gentians, purple of marsh iris; blood red of salvia, magenta of dahlias, yellow of buttercups. Swirling and twisting, they cover the dun sand like a child's finger painting on brown wrapping paper.

Dark green firs add contrast, their needles diamond-tipped from the fog of yesterday. The leaves of birches, softer-hued, pirouette and twinkle.

Like tow-headed boys crowned with red caps, the lighthouses and harbor houses stand proud in the sunlight. Behind them the white clapboard churches and townhalls of the villages dot the landscape.

Birds sing. Gulls chatter. Boats whistle. Fishermen shout. The sun is shining! Surely this mood too was a tentacle which drew Willa Cather to the island.

But the island has one area which is atypical—an area seldom bathed in sunlight. On the

2

rugged west coast, near the northern tip of the oblong land mass lies Dark Harbor. The only road leading to it climbs steeply through dense woods until it comes out suddenly into a wide canyon mouth; then it drops abruptly to the grey sea below. The canyon mouth, with the bit of black beach and narrowly circumscribed harbor, are like a huge bite that has been taken out of the sheer rock walls of the coast.

Dark Harbor is the place of dulse, a species of seaweed which abounds in submarine gardens of the harbor. Though the role of dulse in the life of the island is small, its pungent taste and odor add a strong flavor to the island's personality—a flavor that was not missed by Willa Cather.

This island of light and dark, fog and sun stretches twenty miles from end to end and measures seven miles in breadth at its paunchiest point, four at its narrow waist. The lengthwise miles are linked by a chain of miniature fishing villages which to the outsider are scarcely distinguishable one from the other. From North Head to South Head they extend, following the ins and outs of the coastline—clusters of grey and white houses, with the stinking ash-colored skeletons of wharves and flakes forming a border between them and the sea. Only occasional black lettering on white clapboard proclaiming "Castalia Town Hall" or "Seal Cove Post Office" differentiates a village from its neighbor. No Main Streets intrude: no storefronts obtrude. If a store exists, it hides in the front room of some house that looks like all the other houses. The villagers know its whereabouts. The searching stranger must ask.

Fishing is the island's life blood. It dominates the islanders' life style. It determines their destiny.

Thus the island is a place where menfolk have eyes for little save the sea; a place of weather-beaten countenances and gnarled hands, of muscled arms and sinewy backs. It is a place where hands are seldom idle until the heart is still.

For there is much for hands to do. They set and seine weirs for the herring catch. Or they bait a chain of hooks on a stout trawl line and haul it out to the "grounds," later to be brought in dangling pendants of cod. Or they dot the ocean bed with lobster pots. Or they work in the fish-processing plants or the canneries. In off season, they mend their nets, plying big wooden needles in awkward imitation of their women darning socks; make new lobster pots and repair the old; calk their boats.

Industry was a major tenet of Willa Cather's creed.

But as hands labor, the mind and tongue are not idle. Old stories are swapped: "They say the Indians quit comin' to Indian Beach on account of it's haunted. You wouldn't cetch me down there after dark. Them Indians was smart. They knowed enough to stay away, and that's good enough for me. I ain't hankerin' to see no flamin', burnin' squaw ghost run screamin' down the sands. Besides, they say ever'body ever seen her got overtook with bad luck. I ain't needin' no worse luck than I got."

Droll humor is exchanged, often at the expense of an "outsider." "That book-writin' woman stayin' up to Whale Cove," they used to say, "tells 'em in the bank and the post office: 'You don't pronounce my name "Căther." It's "Cȧther," like "rȧther," the way the English say it.' Haw! Haw! Haw!"

In summer the stories are told on the docks; in winter, around a pot-bellied stove in one of the island's anomalous stores. But summer or winter, the islander is one with the world of waters. He cares about little else. He does not care about authors or the books they write. He does not care about fame. He does not care much about the world "outside."

Individualists, these "herring chokers," courageous and resourceful. Still, they have a unique unity, born not only of their common endeavor but also of their common loss. The waters that surround them are a hard taskmaster that demands many lives. It has been so ever since the ancestors of the present inhabitants, Loyalist refugees from Penobscot, Maine, settled the island at the end of the Revolutionary War.

The island has a long history of discovery. The Pasamaquoddy Indians, who gave it its name, "menan," meaning simply "island," had long since discovered it before Champlain found its rugged coastline in the early years of the 17th Century.

Doubtless its long history, the quality of its people, and its distinct character, as well as its quiet and seclusion each played a part in the appeal it was to have for Willa Cather.

She first learned of the island when she was doing research in the New York Public Library during the winter of 1919-1920. She mentioned to Miss Overton, a librarian there, that an author needed a quiet place to work. Miss Overton had a suggestion. Four of her friends, she said, had vacationed on a small fishing island in the Bay of Fundy and thought it probably the quietest place in the world! One of them, Miss Jacobus, had been so enamored of the island that she had returned and bought property there. Now she had started a small summer place, Whale Cove Inn. Perhaps it would satisfy Miss Cather's needs.

Willa Cather decided to investigate. And so it was that she came to Grand Manan.

She was not disappointed in her "investigation." The appeal of the island was many-faceted, but above all it offered the silence, the solitude, and the seclusion she sought. For the next twenty years she would seek them out again and again.

CHAPTER II

"A little faster, Claude. A little faster," Willa Cather would say to Claude Gilmore, one of two brothers who ran a taxi service on Grand Manan. It was in the early 1920's, and their cab was a Ford touring car. The roads were narrow and winding, and the Islanders were not a speedy breed. The speedometer on the cab would show thirty.

"A little faster," Miss Cather would say.

A little faster. Forty.

The entourage was enroute to Whale Cove from the pier where the boat from the Mainland had deposited Miss Cather and Miss Lewis. Piles of luggage bounced on the running boards and the top of the cab.

Claude Gilmore pursed his lips. The next time she said it...!

"A little faster, Claude," as she clutched at her wide-brimmed hat which the wind was working to unseat.

"We're going over forty, Miss Cather. That's agin' the law. And your bags're bobbin' like buoys. If you wanna get to Whale Cove with 'em, we'd better go a little slower 'stead of a little faster!"

Later, back with his brother Ray, he complained irritably, "What's the matter with the woman?"

Ray only shook his head. He had had similar experiences with "that writin' woman." After a moment's cogitation, he said, "Reckon she's in a hurry to get to work." The brothers chuckled. To them, being in a hurry to get to work was a joke.

Not so to Willa Cather. Unwittingly, Ray Gilmore had hit upon the truth: Miss Cather was always in a hurry to get to her work. And when she arrived at any of her sanctuaries in the Northeast—Grand Manan, New Brunswick; Jaffrey, New Hampshire; or Northeast Harbor, Maine—she was in a hurry for two reasons: She was eager to get to her work and she was eager to get to the haven which was to afford her quiet and privacy in which to do that work. Each of these spots, at different times, knew her devotion. She loved them for their natural beauty, but even more, for the opportunity they afforded her to work undistracted at her writing, for her writing was her life.

At the time Willa Cather started spending summers on Grand Manan, she had already published one volume of poems, one of short stories, and four novels: *Alexander's Bridge, O Pioneers! The Song of the Lark,* and *My Antonia.*

She never drove a car. Having someone else drive with gusto may have been a release for her, a reversal of the way she directed her career—with caution, slowly, steadily—a single-purposed mind on a clear, straight road. She had not gone very fast in her literary career. She was thirty years old before her slight volume of poems, *April Twilights*, saw publication. She was nearing forty when her first novel, *Alexander's Bridge*, was brought out by Houghton Mifflin. Even then, she had not attained mature stature in her art. It was not until she turned to her own material, to write of the immigrants who had come to claim "free land" in Nebraska in the last quarter of the Nineteenth Century—Nebraska, where Willa Cather herself grew up—that she came into her own. This she had finally done in *O Pioneers!*, but at age forty. With a late start, she *was* in a hurry to get to her work. It pushed her. And yet never did her writing evidence haste, for she was a careful, painstaking craftsman.

Willa Cather was born to Charles and Mary Virginia Boak Cather in Frederick County, Virginia, in 1873, but she spent only her very young years in this "old" part of the country before being propelled headlong into the very "new" country of the Midwest.

When she was nine years old, her father moved his family from "Willowshade," the comfortable big brick country house in Virginia, to a farming area known as "The Divide," near Red Cloud, Nebraska. He was following his father and his brother George who had "gone west" some years before and found the new life good. The area in which the Cathers settled was known as "The Divide" because it was a wide, fertile plateau which formed the watershed of two rivers, the Blue and the Republican. Settlement in this west-central section of Nebraska had begun only thirteen years prior to the arrival of the Charles Cather family. A bleak frontier landscape with few trees and few houses, a vast vista stretching as far as the eye could see, with no mountains and no hills to cushion the harshness of the distant horizon. This was the scene that met a small girl's eyes and made them grow big with wonder. Being confronted with this violent contrast from what she had known before was like being drenched with ice-cold water. It was a shock from which Willa Cather never recovered—a shock which undoubtedly had much to do with her becoming one of America's outstanding novelists. She had other "shocks" but this was the initial one.

The "free land" in Nebraska and its fertility had drawn many first-generation foreign immigrants, as well as settlers from the Eastern United States. It was to the foreign families: Bohemians, Germans, Danes, Swedes, and French Canadians that this child of Virginia turned in ecstasy and delight. Their living conditions in the new land were as yet primitive. Some lived in soddies, others in caves known as "dug-outs." But they had brought with them cultures and customs so new to the small girl from Virginia who visited them that it was as if she had been turned loose in the animated pages of an encyclopedia. Their stories, their struggles, their characters, their customs were etched on Willa's impressionable mind like line drawings. And in her heart were stored, in close communion with her own emotions, their love and laughter, their hate and fear, their stubborn determination.

It was, indeed, a precious store that filled her heart and mind.

That time of storing was brief, though there were others to come. Charles Cather soon decided that he was not suited to the life of a Midwestern farmer and moved his family into the town of Red Cloud, where he established a land office. Here the Cathers lived in a small rented house, where, with an expanding family, conditions were crowded. However, Willa had a little attic room of her own which she loved because in it she was able to be alone with her thoughts and her dreams.

In Red Cloud she formed attachments which would prove to be life-long friendships. Here she attended school for the first time in her life. In this little frontier town she was far from "culturally deprived." There was an old German music master from whom she took piano lessons (rather unsuccessfully) who told her stories of operas, stories of the great composers, stories of the Old World. And there were her neighbors, the Weiners, who spoke both French and German fluently and who opened their extensive library to Willa. There were Mrs. Eva Case and Mr. and Mrs. A. K. Goudy, kindly, intelligent teachers. And there was "Uncle Billy" Ducker who tutored her in German along with his own daughters. And there were the traveling stock companies who brought "theatre" to the village. And there were the Garbers, an ex-governor and his beautiful young wife, well-to-do, well-educated and cultured, who offered their friendship.

But also there was a type of experience here for Willa Cather which was different from anything she might have known had she remained in the East. There was freedom—the freedom to explore the little islands in the Republican River; freedom to climb a bluff on which an Indian princess and her horse were said to be buried; to run at will and let the wind blow in her hair; freedom to let her mind and her imagination roam with her wandering feet, and everywhere space— space in which to fling wide her arms and listen to what the wind had to say—and to be alone.

Willa was one of three graduates from the Red Cloud High School in the Class of 1890. In September of that year, she was enrolled in the Preparatory School of the University of Nebraska at Lincoln. This was an opportunity offered pupils whose previous schooling did not quite fit them for University entrance. Willa's formal educational background had been extremely sketchy, but after a year in the Preparatory School, she was admitted to regular University standing. Although she entered with the idea of preparing for a medical career, she soon deserted science for literature. It was in her freshman year that Professor Hunt of the English Department submitted a theme of hers on Carlyle, which he thought remarkably good, to the editor of *The Lincoln State Journal.* The editor also thought it remarkably good and ran it along with a laudatory editorial note. Willa Cather had taken the first small step in her literary career.

She was graduated from the University of Nebraska in June of 1895, and by that time she had seen thousands of words penned by Willa Cather in the paper which had first put her in print. In her junior year, she had begun doing a column, chiefly devoted to dramatic criticism, and through it the name of Willa Cather had become well known

11

locally—sometimes as "that young upstart." She had pulled no punches.

In Red Cloud she had been known as something of a maverick, with her bobbed hair and occasional cigarette and unfeminine attire. In the University it was the same, although an adult friend persuaded her to let her hair grow. She wrote for and edited student publications. Though she was admired for her ability, she made few friends due to her outspokeness and her lack of interest in the trivia of social intercourse.

Following her graduation, came a year spent between Lincoln and Red Cloud, when she was writing not only for the *Journal*, but also for *The Courier*, both Lincoln papers. It was through her journalistic contacts in Lincoln that she was offered her first position, the editorship of a small, new Presbyterian magazine, *The Home Monthly*, in Pittsburgh. At the end of one year in this position, she left the magazine for a job on the *Pittsburgh Leader*, the city's largest newspaper. Here she remained for four years, during the latter part of which her writing began to appear in other publications.

Because she wanted more time to pursue her "private" writing, she left the *Leader* for a position teaching high school Latin and English. This meant longer weekends plus summer vacations in which to write.

It was during her first year of teaching that she met a young woman named Isabelle McClung, whose friendship was to mean a great deal to her. The relationship was based on a community of thinking and of interests. Miss McClung was the daughter of a judge; the family was an old one, highly respected and affluent. Isabelle had been born to Society. However, she found the life boring. The arts and people involved in them had become her chief interests. She invited Willa Cather to leave her boarding house and live in the McClung home. Willa accepted.

Now she was in the kind of environment in which she reveled and in which she felt she belonged. She remained with the McClungs for the rest of her five-year teaching career, which completed her time in Pittsburgh.

After Publisher S. S. McClure had accepted several of her stories for publication in his magazine, he brought out her first volume of prose, a collection of short stories. Then he went to Pittsburgh and offered her an editorial position on *McClure's Magazine.*

This new position took Willa Cather to New York. The year was 1906; she was thirty-three years old. She remained with the magazine five years. During this time, she took up residence with Edith Lewis, whom she had met in Lincoln. The two women lived together the rest of Miss Cather's life.

Finally, at age thirty-eight, she felt sufficiently secure in her writing career to sever her last "job" connections and devote full time to writing.

What was she like? This woman who as a child had been transplanted from the wooded hills of Virginia to the plains of Nebraska; who now had been transplanted from the wide open spaces of the Midwest to the skyscraper canyons of Mid-Manhattan? Brown-haired, blue-eyed, rather stocky in build. Not beautiful but by some termed "handsome." Vigorous. In her prime. An enigma

13

to some. A joy to others. A person of marked likes and dislikes. One who generated strong reactions in those who knew her polar reactions.

When she returned to Nebraska for frequent visits, there were people who referred to her as "that snooty Willa Cather"; those who said she could not see them but elbowed them off the sidewalk. Then there were her good friends, the "foreigners" on the Divide, who truly loved her, and whom she was to help time and again, notably during the depression years. There were, also, friends in town, staunch friends since childhood; these included Carrie Miner Sherwood, who cherished her.

In New York she had a circle of friends, largely authors and musicians. One of her writer friends, Elizabeth Sergeant, saw her "whole." She saw her potential, she admired her; yet she also thought her selfish and often insensitive to the needs of others. Those who courted her as a coming celebrity and those who contacted her for memberships in organizations or for funds for charities were coldly shunted off. She seemed a woman of many faces.

But to all who knew her, either casually or well, it became increasingly apparent that she took herself and her art very seriously. She would allow no intrusions to interfere with them. She was making a name for herself in the literary world. Above all, she wanted quiet and privacy in which to work.

As she acquired even greater success, and with it, greater means, she began to search out places where the environment suited these requirements. She found them in the Northeast: in Jaffrey, on Grand Manan Island, and in Northeast Harbor. All had the same attraction. In these quiet, secluded spots, she was to spend several months of each year—the summers and the autumns.

CHAPTER III

In her quest, the first such haven Willa Cather found, preceding her discovery of Grand Manan by five years, was a village in New Hampshire, a village founded exactly one hundred years before her birth and given the name of Jaffrey Center. With the Contoocook River meandering through the wooded hills, and backed by the rock mass known as Mt. Monadnock, it was a natural spot for a summer resort. A summer resort Jaffrey became, one of the first in New Hampshire.

Early in the planning and building of any New England village was the all-important Meeting House. So in the early days of summer, 1775, when the cannon were booming at Bunker Hill eighty miles away, a large frame Meeting House with an impressive Christopher Wren tower, unusual in that it was unattached, was "raised" in Jaffrey Center. This accomplished, a low, dozen-stall stable was built behind it, for when a man came to meeting his horse must have shelter. Soon thereafter came the first burial in the cemetery behind the Meeting House, the cemetery which was later to receive the remains of Amos Fortune, who had bought his freedom from enforced

15

slavery, and still later, of Willa Cather, who was always in voluntary bondage.

Some three winding wooded miles east of Jaffrey Center a little industry began to develop on the river, and a limited business district grew. For a time, this area was known as "East Jaffrey", but by the time Willa Cather came to summer in the shadow of Mt. Monadnock, it was simply "Jaffrey." With Jaffrey Center, population 300, it formed a unit, though with two separate post offices. It was a lovely, quiet, peaceful town of stately Colonial homes surrounded by spacious sloping lawns splotched with pools of shade, and of "hostelries" in park-like settings so that memories of the crowded cities from which guests came faded as they gazed on wooded acres or watched the sunset beyond Mt. Monadnock.

It was into this setting that Willa Cather stepped one summer day in 1917, and, obsessed as she was with a desire for privacy and a quiet place in which to write, it was not surprising that this proved to be only the first of many visits she was to make.

There were two drawing cards to bring her to Jaffrey that first summer: Her good friend Isabelle McClung Hambourg and her husband were staying at the Shattuck Inn, and two Pittsburgh friends, the Misses Lucy Hind and Ethel Acheson, were spending the summer at High Mowing, a summer home they had rented about a mile from the Shattuck.

Willa Cather and Isabelle McClung had been very close in the years following Isabelle's invitation to live in the McClung home and Willa's acceptance. Willa had shared Isabelle's room on the second floor, and a little attic room had been prepared as a writing nook for her. Long evenings the two young women had spent together reading Flaubert and other favorite authors. They had attended the theatre and concerts together. Willa had made her first trip abroad accompanied by Isabelle. And when she finally decided to break away from her editorial position with *McClure's Magazine,* Isabelle had gone with her to Cherry Valley in Upper New York, where they had rented a house for several months, and Willa had had her first taste of a secluded place for writing. Often too, in the years before Judge McClung's death, after Willa had moved to New York, she spent months at a time at Murray Hill in Pittsburgh. Thus it was a real shock to her, the second violent shock of her life, when Isabelle, after her father's death, chose to marry Violinist Jan Hambourg. There is little doubt that Willa Cather had expected Isabelle to remain at Murray Hill, to offer her sanctuary when she wished it, to be available to go with her where and when she desired. But when Isabelle married, she gave up the family home in Pittsburgh and was never to know a really permanent home again, traveling with her husband wherever his music dictated. So an anchor was weighed, and the embarkation into strange waters was for Willa Cather a traumatic experience.

Nonetheless, the friendship between the two women was not severed, and whenever proximity made it feasible, the Hambourgs and Willa visited.

It was simply for a holiday, then, that Willa Cather first came to Jaffrey, New Hampshire. She had taken the train from New York to Boston, where she changed to the "Boston and Maine" for Jaffrey. She enjoyed train rides, and this one took

17

her through country where she had been only once—ten years before, when she had first started to work for Sam McClure.

As an early assignment, McClure had sent her to Boston to continue research for a revealing article on Mary Baker Eddy, upon which one of his other writers had embarked, only to become shipwrecked. While most of her time on this assignment was spent in Boston, she had made some excursions to New Hampshire—to the village of Bow, where Mary Baker Eddy was born, and to Concord where she later lived. Willa had enjoyed New England, its landscape and a number of its people. As setting and character were always important to her, she was glad now of the opportunity to become better acquainted with New England's treasures.

It was in Boston that she had met Sarah Orne Jewett, the author of *The Country of the Pointed Firs* and other fine New England stories. Now as the train swung through the wooded Massachusetts hills, she was sharply reminded of Miss Jewett's influence upon her own career.

It was Sarah Orne Jewett who had advised her to give up her editorial duties at McClure's and devote full time to writing and who had admonished her to "find her own quiet center of life...and write from that." Though she did not take Miss Jewett's advice at once, eventually she did leave McClure's. And, starting with the long short story, "The Bohemian Girl," published five years before her first visit to Jaffrey, she had written from her own quiet center of life. She had written of life on "The Divide" in Nebraska, her feeling for the country and the immigrants who

18

settled it. She had followed "The Bohemian Girl" with the novel, *O Pioneers!*, in which she had continued to follow Miss Jewett's advice; with its publication she took her place among the major fiction writers of the time.

Now she was launched on another novel in which she was again using her own material, and even though the Jaffrey outing was supposed to be a holiday, she brought with her the manuscript on which she was working.

The village of Jaffrey, she thought, as she was driven through it, differed little in its size and unpretentious appearance from the Red Cloud of her young years. The difference lay rather in the contour of the land—rolling hills in place of flat plains—and in the abundance of trees which darkened every hill in and around Jaffrey. She sniffed the smell of pines appreciatively. There was something that drew her to villages.

Many years later, Pearl Buck was to say: "The key to great civilizations lies far from the cities ....The life blood of a nation is fed from its villages." Certainly American culture was portrayed through Willa Cather's fine literary prose for much of its material had to do with life in the nation's villages, and much of it was written in remote and quiet ones.

The Shattuck Inn proved to be a large, three-story, white frame structure, not beautiful in itself but in a beautiful setting. With its annex and four guest cottages, it could house two hundred people. It was filled nearly to capacity when Willa Cather arrived, but there was a small dormer room available on the third floor which she engaged. It would not have been considered desirable by most but it suited her well. It was one of the least expensive rooms in the Inn. It was reached by a narrow, cage-like "lift," operated by the bellboy. There was one small window at the end of the room, and a larger one, a bay, in the sloping roof on the north, at the rear of the Inn. Both looked out on fields divided and rimmed with stone fences, fringed with pine woods, and back-dropped by Mt. Monadnock.

The room was a logical choice—as far as possible from other guests, it would be a quiet place. But was there more? Had she unconsciously chosen a dormer room because it was reminiscent of the attic room of her childhood in Red Cloud, Nebraska? As a girl, she had loved to listen to the rain on the loft roof; and on clear nights, she had felt close to the stars and the heavens. Nor was this time in Jaffrey to be the last in which she would seek and find a dormer room in which to live and/or write.

Her name did not appear on the Shattuck register that year nor in subsequent years. This was another evidence of her desire for privacy.

The Shattuck Inn, at the time of Miss Cather's arrival, was relatively new. The original structure, converted from a large country house about 1869, when Mrs. Edmund P. Shattuck began taking in summer boarders, had been enlarged twice before fire destroyed it in 1909. After the fire, the Shattuck's son, then manager, immediately rebuilt, and on July 1, 1910, opened the new Inn which housed a hundred guests. Two years later he built an addition, and the following year an annex, doubling capacity.

So, although the building in which she was

housed was less than ten years old when Willa Cather came to the Shattuck, the Inn as an establishment for summer residents had been well known in New England for forty years. Its atmosphere was one of gentility. Its clientele was quality. Many of its guests returned regularly, year after year. Many of them were "little old ladies." There was often entertainment in the evenings, with musical groups such as a stringed trio performing. The food was excellent, home cooking all the way—from the Saturday night-Sunday morning baked beans to the Indian pudding and freezer ice cream. All of these things Willa Cather liked: an atmosphere of gentility, music, cultured elderly ladies, good food. But even more she embraced the privacy of her little room under the eaves.

However, the days could become uncomfortably warm in Jaffrey in August, and the summer sun on the slanting roof over Miss Cather's room did not make for ideal writing conditions. She wanted to get on with the novel she had begun. It was needling her. Afternoons and evenings she would be glad to spend with her friends, but mornings she wanted to write.

The ladies at High Mowing offered a solution: Pitch a tent in their meadow! Willa Cather thought High Mowing an enchanting spot. Its house stood high on a hill at the end of a long lane off Thorndike Pond Road. There was always a breeze. There were sloping hills and jig-saw meadows, all surrounded by a desultory stone wall.

The tent was pitched. It was furnished with a table and camp chair. Willa Cather was in business.

She ate a hearty breakfast each morning in the Shattuck dining room, collected her writing materials from her room, went through the kitchen to pick up two doughnuts for munching in mid-morning, and started her half-mile hike to the High Mowing meadow. She wore sturdy, high, laced shoes, a dark skirt that just met her shoe-tops, and a long-sleeved middy blouse. She gave no thought to appearance as she strode on her way. Her mind was on the chapter on which she would soon be working.

The tone of the book was quiet, like the countryside in which it was being composed. Willa Cather was always strongly influenced by place and she was at peace in Jaffrey.

She could catch the scent of pine in her meadow studio. There were days in which the fragrance of new-mown hay added a subtle pleasure. And always there was the impress of the mountain hovering near—Monadnock. It was an Indian name, she had been told, meaning "The Place of the Great Spirit." Was that why it seemed to be a source of inspiration? A rock, really, a mass of rock. "How firm a foundation . . ." It seemed to give one spiritual strength. The writing went well.

When the period of vacationing was over for the Hambourgs, Miss Cather decided to stay on. She was no longer vacationing. She was working. Working with very satisfying results. Why leave?

As the heat of summer receded and the bracing air of autumn took its place, as the red and gold of fall foliage patterned the deep green of pine, and summer guests departed, the Shattuck became ideally quiet. Everything was working now to the artist's advantage. She had found an ideal autumn retreat with an atmosphere that sometimes reminded her of a cathedral. Here she was stimulated, yet quiet; here she had found the privacy which she desired.

She would return again and again to the sanctuary offered by Jaffrey and its massive mountain.

CHAPTER IV

Although Willa Cather saw more and more of Jaffrey each mid-September to late November during the next twenty years, people saw less and less of Willa Cather either in Jaffrey or elsewhere. Even her traditional Friday afternoon teas in her New York apartment were discontinued.

To some it seemed that World War I was the cause of her withdrawal. With it she considered the world to have "broken in two." She was disgruntled with society, so she cut herself off from it. But there were those who thought that, while becoming disenchanted with the world, Willa Cather had conversely become more enchanted with herself. There were still others who ascribed her isolation to the fact that she was saving herself for her work.

All three of these views could be found in Jaffrey. The "little old ladies" who were regular guests at the Inn generally concurred with the first conclusion. Tradespeople in the village were more of the second opinion. They had their reasons. For instance, Edith Lewis always made Miss Cather's

23

appointments with the hairdresser under some other name than Cather. This the beauty operators considered an unnecessary bit of tomfoolery indicative of Miss Cather's exaggerated sense of self-importance.

Notable among persons holding the third view as to the reason for the author's withdrawal was Edith Lewis. Others such as the Shattucks and Austermanns were inclined to agree.

As was to become true on Grand Manan, there were those in Jaffrey who made jokes about Miss Cather and her "strange ways." She insisted, for example, upon a coiled rope by the window of her room at the Shattuck. While some said she had a phobia about fires and others pointed out that it was only common sense to take such precautions in a room such as hers, the younger employees at the Inn considered the rope a source of great amusement.

Willa Cather, then in her forties, was stocky of build, and when one of the maids said, "Can you imagine her wriggling through that little window?" gales of laughter followed.

"Imagine the 'Old Pioneer' slithering down a rope!" another chimed in.

"Three stories down! Wouldn't that be the cat's meow?"

But the general attitude of Jaffrey was to ignore the famous author in their midst, leaving her to her own devices and business.

Her business at the moment was the story of Annie Sadilek. She worked on it both in Jaffrey and New York—despite the great contrast in her surroundings. In New York her writing room faced a concrete wall a few feet away. Thus she imposed

24

silence and solitude upon herself. In the Northeast, silence and solitude were voluntary companions.

In Jaffrey she was invariably up early and soon at work in her study in the pines or in the tent at High Mowing. When the story of Annie Sadilek was finished, under the title of *My Antonia*, it was at Jaffrey that she and Edith Lewis read the galley proofs. She was pleased with the book, and her judgment of it was sound. By many it is considered her best novel.

While most of the autumn days in Jaffrey were fair, there were occasional rainy ones. It was during one such period that Miss Cather contracted influenza. Dr. Frederick Sweeney was called to attend her, and in the course of her illness he made several calls at the Shattuck. As her condition improved, doctor and patient had several mutually enjoyable conversations, discovering that they had a number of common interests.

At one point Dr. Sweeney mentioned that he had been the sole doctor on a troopship in the First World War, when an epidemic of influenza broke out. This particularly interested Willa Cather because she was now working on a novel set during the war. In fact, she had just reached a point in the story where information about troop transport was needed and was wondering where she could find it.

As they continued to talk, Dr. Sweeney confided that he had kept a diary of the voyage. Miss Cather asked if she might read it, but he demurred, saying it was too personal. Undaunted, she proceeded to persuade until he finally loaned her the diary. She did not tell him her reason for wanting to read it.

A few days later she returned it, thanking him for the loan.

One of Ours, the World War I story, appeared in 1922. The protagonist, Claude Wheeler, was a misfit on a Midwest farm who felt he found his niche in the war in France. Miss Cather had made abundant use of Dr. Sweeney's diary in the portion of the book dealing with Claude's crossing the Atlantic via troop ship.

The novel of course came to the attention of Dr. Sweeney who easily recognized himself and the troopship of his diary. He was angry, considering that his confidence had been betrayed. When he learned that Willa Cather was returning to the Shattuck Inn, he ascertained the time of her arrival and was waiting in the lobby to confront her when she walked in.

The first thing she saw on entering was his angry face, and she had the grace to blush and attempt a stuttered apology. It was difficult, however, to explain why she had not asked his permission to use material from his diary. He surmised correctly that she had not asked because she thought he would refuse.

Later, peace was made between the two and their friendship continued until the doctor's death. Indeed, the Sweeney Family became proud that the doctor and his diary had thus been used and given a commanding audience. The diary is now on loan to the Clay Library in Jaffrey.

It was while she was in Jaffrey that Miss Cather received notice that the American Academy of Arts and Letters had awarded her the William Dean Howells Medal for Fiction. She did not, however, attend the ceremony. She hated crowds. So instead of dignitaries, it was a bellboy, having collected her mail at the Jaffrey post office, who presented the award to her.

When weather permitted—and it usually did—Willa Cather took walks in the afternoons. This was a pastime she followed most of her life and Jaffrey was a pleasing place to pursue it. Sometimes she was taken for drives—to the Poole Reservation; to Peterborough, near where the MacDowell Colony was located; most frequently to Mt. Monadnock, "The Mountain that Stands Alone" or "The Place of the Great Spirit." Though Willa Cather had frequented the Rockies and the Alps, Monadnock gave her a special spiritual uplift as it hovered like a sentinel two thousand feet above the quiet town. Ten trails lead to Mt. Monadnock, and Willa Cather frequented all of them.

One reason she preferred Jaffrey in the fall was that there were fewer people there then; in the summers the population of the area doubled. In autumn it was easier to find the quiet and seclusion she sought—until the autumn of 1938.

Two enormous storms shook the Western World on September 21 that year: One was the Czechoslovakian Government's surrender to "irresistible pressure" and agreement to cede its predominantly Germanic Sudetan areas to Germany. It was said that this was "a sellout," that the plan was "the destruction and mutilation of a sovereign state," that it would lead to "incalculable and disastrous consequences" sooner or later.

But the destruction and mutilation of the second storm were immediate. Seven states in Northeast U. S. A. were struck by a tropical hurricane. Savage one-hundred-mile-an-hour winds raged in the worst storm to hit the North Atlantic for a century. Panic seized citizens as it broke all records for rapidity of movement and continued intensity. It took nearly seven hundred lives. It injured thousands.

For two days Vermont and New Hampshire were lost in the silence of broken communication systems. Jaffrey and vicinity were included. Then, via ham radio, came pleas from Peterborough, seven miles from Jaffrey, for help in fighting fires that had broken out, but roads were submerged and impassable. No help could get through. Highways, bridges, telephone and electric wires and gas lines had been ripped apart over many square miles. Sea going and small craft by the hundred had been lost, sunk, or driven ashore. Buildings demolished. Farms and families marooned. The loss was inestimable. Homes and cottages collapsed into dreary piles of kindling. Whole forests had been uprooted.

Including Willa Cather's "cathedral."

This holocaust, in the autumn of the year, occurred in the autumn of Willa Cather's life. She never returned there. Her love affair with Jaffrey had lasted twenty-one years.

In the autumn of 1929, nine years before her visits to Jaffrey came to an end, a four-year-old twin son of George and Eleanor (Shattuck) Austermann died. On a rainy day, his remains were placed in the Old Burying Ground.

Willa Cather attended the services. She regarded the grave. She listened. All was quiet, peaceful. She looked. Mt. Monadnock, towering, stood to the northwest, on guard. Possibly it was

28

then that the thought first came to her: "This might be the place...to be when the time comes."

CHAPTER V

"In the life of each of us," wrote Sarah Orne Jewett, friend and mentor of Miss Cather, "there is a place remote and islanded."

Literally, this place existed for Willa Cather on the Island of Grand Manan. It was not that she had crossed Jaffrey off her list, when, in the summer of 1922, she and Edith Lewis packed for the train trip to Boston on the first leg of their first journey to Grand Manan. There were, in fact, sixteen years remaining, during which she would spend time in Jaffrey. It was simply that Miss Jacobus' enthusiasm for this little New Brunswick island, her description of the isolation of Whale Cove, her mention of the wild flowers, and the impression she gave of its remoteness—all relayed by Librarian Overton—had whetted Miss Cather's curiosity and had intrigued her to the point where she must see for herself.

It was not a simple matter to get from New York to Grand Manan. A less determined woman might well have given up the quest after investigating the way one must go. But Willa Cather was never easily daunted and if a destination seemed likely to be desirable, especially in furthering her career, no obstacle was too great for her to hurdle.

Even before leaving New York she knew there would be obstacles: (1) the necessity of changing from train to boat in Boston; and (2) the necessity of changing from one boat to another at Eastport, Maine. Not anticipated: (1) the poor accommodations on the boats; (2) the early-morning arrival of Boat Number One at Eastport; and (3) the long, indeterminate wait—sans accommodations—in Eastport for Boat Number Two.

With Edith Lewis and all their baggage, at four o'clock on a raw, foggy morning, Willa Cather found herself on the wharf at Eastport. A few other passengers had also disembarked; some had disappeared into the gloom, but two or three remained, obviously waiting, as were Miss Cather and Miss Lewis, for the Grand Manan boat. A shed-like ticket office, containing a plank bench, was the only semblance of a waiting room. The few passengers sat down on the bench to wait.

"You might see when the boat is expected," Miss Cather said to Miss Lewis, who got up without a word and went to the ticket window.

"They don't know," she reported.

"*Don't know?*" Miss Cather repeated with raised eyebrows.

"That's what he said."

The wait went on and on. The air was chill and the atmosphere was even chillier. Miss Cather pulled her coat collar up. Now and then she would turn her head and give her companion a look which would again send Edith Lewis to the ticket window, but the response was always the same, and Miss Lewis, returning, would shake her head.

Fragments of conversation from the other waiting passengers reached the ears of the two women:

"You've never been to Grand Manan before?... You're going for a *holiday*?... *Why* would anyone go to that fog factory if he didn't have to?"

"Doesn't this boat run on a regular schedule?"

"Schedule?!" Sarcastic laugh. "They never even heard of a schedule. The boat may be in sometime this morning—*later* this morning... Much later... Maybe..."

The women from New York took no part in this discussion. They spoke to no one but each other, and then only in monosyllables. Finally Miss Cather stood up and paced—strode—back and forth on the wharf. Miss Lewis stayed with all of their baggage.

At long last a croaking, fog-choked whistle sounded in the distance. The passengers began to stir. One said in a worried tone, "Mr. Jones walked up to the hotel. Do you suppose he'll hear the whistle? They'll go off without him if he isn't here when she docks. They never wait a minute."

"Wouldn't wait for God Almighty."

Miss Cather helped gather up the numerous pieces of luggage at Miss Lewis' feet, as it was obvious that there was no one available to carry it for them, and the two, with Miss Cather leading the way, went down the gang-plank to the boat which would take them on the last lap of their journey.

Miss Cather was a good sailor; Miss Lewis was not. It was always with trepidation that Miss Lewis stepped onto a boat. This one was not large. Tales of the roughness of the seas around Grand Manan had already reached the women's ears. Miss Lewis gritted her teeth, but Miss Cather watched the sun disperse the fog and waited expectantly for her first view of the island.

After two hours of steady chugging, the boat brought them in sight of a lighthouse, stark white, high on a cliff. The dark outline of land began to take shape. They were approaching Grand Manan.

Almost unbelievably, there was a taxi at the wharf. Not that it displayed the word, "TAXI," nor that its driver was in uniform. Nonetheless, a tall, gaunt man approached the two women as they struggled off the boat with their baggage, and asked, "Taxi, Ladies?"

"Please," Miss Lewis said. And when they were loaded into the Ford touring car, she appended, "Whale Cove Cottage."

After a mile or two, the driver broke the silence. "So you ladies are a goin' to 'The Dovecote'?"

No response.

The road they took for a mile or two followed the shore, though well above it. Looking through trees and down a steep embankment, they could see the waters of the Bay of Fundy. They were close enough to hear it lapping. They passed a few houses, well spaced, an interesting frame church on a hill to their right. A little farther on, they turned off the main thoroughfare—along which ran no sidewalk for the few pedestrians whom they saw. They had met only one car. When they turned off, their driver said, "This here's Whistle Light Road."

A mile or so farther he turned the car into a narrow lane that snaked between tall pines until they were again in sight of shore. "And that's Whale Cove," he said then.

What the two women saw as the car moved down the grassy track was a handful of weather-beaten grey shingle cottages crouching on the edge of the quiet waters of an inlet fringed with marsh grass. Yes, it looked quiet enough and remote enough for Miss Cather's purposes. She was pleased.

Miss Jacobus greeted them effusively but apologetically. As all the rooms in Whale Cove Cottage were occupied by her regular guests who engaged them summer after summer, she would have to put the ladies in another cottage. It was just down the road a short way. It had no modern conveniences, so she didn't know if they would want to stay, but she *would* love to have them.

They looked over the available rooms in the cottage to which she led them, and Miss Cather nodded in satisfaction. This would be better than staying in Whale Cove Cottage with its other guests.

Thus began Miss Cather's first stay on the Island of Grand Manan. She had brought with her the manuscript on which she was working, that of the novel *A Lost Lady*.

"I want it understood that I am to be left alone," she told Miss Jacobus. "I have come here to work. I do not want to be disturbed."

Miss Jacobus assured her that she would tell her other guests of this request. She would see to it that Miss Cather would be left strictly alone. She explained when meals would be served. She then left the two new guests to unpack and store their trappings while she hastened back to tell the waiting ladies all about the exciting new members of the "Colony." She was greatly impressed that her establishment had attracted so famous a person as Willa Cather.

Nearly all of Miss Jacobus' guests were unmarried women, so she referred laughingly to Whale Cove Cottage as her "Home for the Crossed in Love." This was a time when women were feeling new ground, and these women needed no sympathy. They were leading the lives they wanted to lead.

The villagers had nicknamed the establishment "The Dovecote," thinking of its residents as so many little grey doves.

So now the Dovecote's inhabitants fluttered about fluffing their feathers in anticipation of the first meal with their celebrity guest. Even the kitchen help were in a stir, the cook having been given orders to prepare a special meal and the waitresses to give special attention to the table of the two new ladies.

So Kathleen Small, teenage waitress and Miss Jacobus' "right-hand man," stood expectantly by the door between kitchen and dining room as Miss Cather and Miss Lewis entered. What she saw was to her a surprise and a disappointment. In her mind's eye she had seen Miss Cather as similar to Eloise Derby, a guest whom she greatly admired: genteel, charming, lovely to look at. Instead she saw a sturdily built middle-aged woman wearing white gloves and a large sailor hat planted firmly and squarely on her head, who looked neither to right nor left as dourly she followed Miss Jacobus to a table.

The woman with her was smaller, slighter in build, also wearing white gloves, but no hat; her hair was grey, cut short, worn straight. She carried a small coffee pot in her hand and a jar of coffee. These she handed to Miss Jacobus who, as soon as her guests were seated, bustled into the kitchen with the paraphernalia and gave explicit instructions for its use: Miss Cather wanted her own coffee each meal. Here was the coffee and the pot in which to prepare it. They must always be sure to serve it to her piping hot. She liked her coffee *very hot*.

The kitchen contingent quit staring and went into action. These prim women with their prim instructions! And the name on the jar was "Coffee-Hag"! What a giggle-prompting combination!

Miss Cather and Miss Lewis had been seated at a table with two other guests, as the tables in the Whale Cove Cottage dining room were set up for four each. These two companion tablemates had been chosen by Miss Jacobus with care; even so, they did not find it easy to carry on a conversation with the celebrated author and her companion. In fact, the presence of the new guests seemed to foster a feeling of restraint among all of the diners that day. They were inclined to speak in hushed tones, as if awed with the Presence which had descended among them. This, of course, was not to last, at least in this degree. But this was the first day.

Miss Cather, though the guests thought her remote and uncommunicative, was pleased with Whale Cove. The cottage in which she and Miss Lewis had been housed had only two other guests. Separated as it was by tall marsh grass from Whale Cove Cottage, looking out over the sea on one side and a sea of grass on the other, it seemed this should be a good summer. So she did not stop to chat with the others after lunch, when they assembled in the pleasant sitting room at the Cottage. With Miss Lewis at her heels, she marched directly from the dining room, through the sitting room, back to the other cottage.

Sunshine sparkled on the water, a light breeze ruffled the tall grasses and whispered in the pines. Tomorrow she would get to work, but this was a good afternoon for a walk. She suggested it to Miss Lewis. "Get Mathews' *Field Book*," she said. "We'll take it with us." They would look into the purported profusion of wild flowers on the island.

Miss Lewis raised an eyebrow. "It's heavy," she reminded.

"But worth it," Miss Cather replied.

Before they reached the fringe of woods, she scanned the skies, nodded. The sunny day—although the last she would see for some time—seemed a good omen.

CHAPTER VI

As the summer progressed, it appeared that Miss Overton had been correct in her estimate of Grand Manan Island as "a quiet place in which an author could work." The day in New York when she spoke of the Island to Miss Cather proved during the summer of '22 to be an auspicious one for the author. And so Miss Cather and Miss Lewis returned the next summer and the next to Miss Jacobus' haven.

After a hearty breakfast at Whale Cove Cottage, which always included four slices of underdone bacon "like the English do it," Miss Cather retreated to her room where she wrote until lunch time. *A Lost Lady* had been completed during the winter following her first summer on Grand Manan; during the second summer she was immersed in a new book, *The Professor's House*. It was so quiet in the cottage that she could hear the scratch of her own pen. There were no interruptions: no telephone jangling, no messenger boy ringing a doorbell, no deliveries, not even a postman bringing mail. None of Miss Jacobus' other guests ever stopped by Miss Cather's quarters for a chat. Not only had they taken Miss Jacobus at her word when she told them they were not to "bother" the author; Miss Cather's own behavior was a frosty deterrent to social intercourse.

What the other ladies could not understand was why she felt it necessary to be so aloof at meals. At the Cather-Lewis table, the other two women who made up the foursome were frequently changed. The way Miss Derby expressed it, "After a short time they were always dismissed." When it came time for Miss Derby and Miss Frith to take their turn, things went well for a couple of days. The four of them talked of Paris "and restaurants and that kind of thing." Then Miss Frith made a fatal mistake. She asked if the incident of a boy's putting out the eyes of a bird in *A Lost Lady* were true. Miss Cather froze. "And," said Miss Derby, "that was the end of us."

As summer followed summer, matters did not change. It appeared to the other guests at Whale

Cove that Miss Cather was unnecessarily cautious in avoiding people and unduly concerned with protecting herself. Couldn't she see that they were little concerned with Willa Cather, author? The summer people, having once understood that she wanted privacy, would not intrude upon it. And certainly the Island people were not autograph hunters.

Thus people were inclined to think her haughty and egotistical. Inevitably there were incidents about which some chortled, especially incidents in which she appeared to be trying to hide her identity. There was a story, for example, about a woman and her daughter who had just arrived on the island and were taking a walk.

"We saw this woman in the woods," the mother said, "and were greatly relieved, for we were really lost. We didn't know one direction from another. The woman was a little way off the path, so I called to her. 'I wonder if you could help us,' I said. 'We've lost our direction and don't know how to get back to the road.'

"Then a very queer thing happened. She answered me, but she turned her head away from us as if she thought we were on the other side of her. She gave us directions, but all the time she stood with her head twisted away from us. When we got back to the inn where we were staying, I told the story, saying we couldn't understand this strange behavior. The guests began to laugh. 'That would be Willa Cather,' they said. 'She didn't want you to know you were talking to the great author!'"

As time went on this story was told and retold, growing with each repetition until at last, told to regale the loiterers in North Head's General Store, it included the woman and daughter's getting lost in the woods a second time. Again they came upon "the strange woman"; again they asked directions; again she gave them, but this time with head turned so far away from them that they were sure her neck was double-jointed.

But Miss Cather was not one of the loiterers in the General Store. She appeared there only occasionally with Miss Lewis. More often Miss Lewis was alone. When someone inquired of her about her friend, her answer was always the same: Miss Cather was working. The Islanders understood that Miss Lewis had a position with a publishing house in New York, but they wondered how she could retain it when she spent months at a time away from it with Miss Cather.

At Whale Cove Cottage, by the third summer of Miss Cather's retreat to the Island, the author with her peculiarities was taken for granted, and her habits no longer made a stir among the other guests. "She was temperamental, as we assumed creative people had a right to be," one said. They respected her privacy but thought her unnecessarily distant in her relations with people. "She was very curious," said Eloise Derby. "She could be delightful and agreeable when she wanted. She had all kinds of peculiarities, though. She was difficult about the quiet and difficult about the food. Miss Jacobus, for one, could find her very difficult."

Miss Jacobus' "help" also found her difficult. Besides Kathleen Small there was another waitress named Kathleen whose last name was Smith. Kathleen Smith said, "Her plate usually went back to the kitchen two or three times. Either the food was too hot or too cold, or too much or too little."

Some of the personnel dreaded the time each year when the Cather-Lewis contingent departed for their return to New York. It meant that "the help" had to be up half the night to get them off, for they took the six a.m. boat on a Friday, and breakfast must be served to them before they left. "It was only on Fridays that the boat made this early run," Kathleen Small remembered. "But I guess the early start fit in with the rest of their schedule. Anyway they always took it."

Another situation that "the help" failed to appreciate occurred each time Miss Jacobus' guests were given a picnic lunch to eat in some attractive outdoor setting. While all the other guests participated in these excursions, Miss Cather and Miss Lewis did not, making it necessary for at least one member of the kitchen staff to remain at Whale Cove to prepare and serve their meal.

"Miss Cather seemed very careful about staying away from people," according to Kathleen Small. "She seemed to fear they would ask questions about her books and take her time. She didn't have to be afraid of that on this island!"

Looking back on those days in the 1920's when Whale Cove was host to the author, she shook her head. "Strange," she said. "She wasn't at all sympathetic about people in real life, yet she could be very sympathetic about people in her books."

The fact remained, however, that her chosen way of sequestered solitude and undisturbed quiet resulted in books of high literary merit, and that those books had a charming quietude of their own. It was probably necessary for Willa Cather to husband herself for her work, as Miss Lewis explained she must do, in order to produce her art. The island folk simply thought she overdid it. "If he (the writer)," Miss Cather said in the Preface she wrote for the collection of Sarah Orne Jewett's stories published by Houghton Mifflin in 1925, "achieves anything noble, anything enduring, it must be by giving himself absolutely to his material." Giving herself absolutely to her material seemed to mean largely shutting out the world around her. Hers was a single direction.

So came the summer of 1925. That year, when Miss Cather and Miss Lewis took their afternoon walks, they had something more in mind than identifying wild flowers. They were thinking of building a cottage of their own on Grand Manan, and they were looking for a likely spot.

Earlier Miss Cather had considered buying a summer home at Jaffrey, even having gone so far as to make an appointment with the Robertsons, who owned High Mowing, to talk about buying that property. But when the time came for the meeting, she had found some excuse not to go. Making decisions that involved change was difficult for her.

However, on the matter of a summer place on Grand Manan, she finally came to a decision. She would have one built on the plan of the Jacobus cottage in which she roomed.

Finding the proper lot was important. She had become fond of Whale Cove and wanted to build in that area. She wanted a view of the Bay.

In the summer of 1925 they found what she

wanted. It was about a quarter of a mile from Miss Jacobus' property. Miss Lewis went into action, and the following summer a lot was purchased.

This, of course, was only the beginning. The lot was in deep woods and must be cleared, not only space for the cottage, but also the area between it and the Bay so the view would not be obscured. The lot was twenty feet above the water, with a steep incline dropping to the water's edge.

While Miss Cather continued to work on *The Professor's House*, Miss Lewis secured workmen to clear the lot, then a contractor to build the cottage. Miss Cather laid out the exact spot where it was to stand, facing the water. The living room would be on the front. There would be two bedrooms, a kitchen, and a small washroom, and above the whole, an open attic. There were to be back-to-back fireplaces, one in the living room, the other in the larger of the two bedrooms. (This bedroom would be Miss Lewis's. Miss Cather, as usual, took the smaller one for herself.) There were no plans for a bathroom; no wiring to be done for electricity; no telephone line to be brought in. The new cottage was to be as primitive as the century-old one after which it was fashioned. The exterior was to be of shingles, matching the other Whale Cove cottages.

The lot required some grading after the necessary clearing had been done, and the result was a sharp drop at the back, quite close to where the rear wall of the cottage would go. The contractor shook his head, but Miss Cather could see nothing wrong with her plan. "We will just build a wall back there," she said, "a wall of native stone. It will be very picturesque." It was not the looks but the practicality with which the contractor was concerned, but he would follow her wishes. It was not until some years later that the logic of his objection was proved to be correct.

"We would like to have it ready to move into next summer when we come," Miss Cather said. So lumber was brought in from the mainland and work began that summer.

Each time she walked through the woods from the Jacobus' cottage to her lot, Willa Cather experienced mounting excitement. At first it was so quiet she could hear her own breathing. The only other sound was the sweet trill of a wren high in some hidden treetop. As she came closer, she heard the ring of axe, and she quickened her pace. Then came the cough of the motors and the rasp of saws.

It would be good to have a place of her own! A place she knew she could return to each summer, with no one else anywhere near, no one but Edith Lewis who knew her place, who knew her part. Quiet upon quiet. It had taken her a long time to come to this decision, and it had been difficult, but she felt sure that it was right.

CHAPTER VII

In the summer of 1927 Miss Cather's and Miss Lewis's dream of their own summer home became a reality. This did not happen without struggle, however. The two New Yorkers floundered through such problems as getting water for their cottage and obtaining furniture for it. It had been a simple matter to turn a faucet in the New York apartment to get a drink, to visit a department store to purchase a needed rug or chair.

On Grand Manan a well must be put down to secure water, and even after men had been found to drill, there were problems. At a depth of fifty feet they struck water, but they did not think it would be adequate. Six feet farther down the drill struck the vein for which they were probing and water gushed out like a geyser. Now another project had to be undertaken, the construction of a large concrete tank to contain the water and from which it would be pumped to the cottage.

Then came the problem of furnishing their new home. A couple of colorful Navajo rugs which Miss Cather had obtained in the Southwest and a trunkful of bedding had been shipped out from New York. But other necessities such as a kitchen range, an ice box, a table and chairs, and beds all must be obtained on the Mainland. It took most of that first summer for the two women to get settled in.

Long before this process was completed, however, Miss Cather was in the attic with her Oliver typewriter and her manuscript of *Death Comes for the Archbishop*.

Downstairs, she realized, help was needed. She had observed with favor a young man who occasionally helped Miss Jacobus with repair work or other jobs requiring a man's strong arm. His name was Ralph Beal. He was a fisherman, tall and well built, quiet, well-mannered and pleasant. Upon inquiry Miss Cather found that he lived on Whistle Road not far from her and that he had a healthy young wife. If she could secure the pair of them, the husband for the outdoor work and heavier chores, the wife for cleaning and laundry, life would be much easier for her and Miss Lewis pioneering in their woodland cottage.

One afternoon when she was taking a walk, she met a young woman pushing a baby carriage.

"Are you Ralph Beal's wife?" she asked the young woman without preamble.

Aggie Beal recognized Willa Cather and was quite overwhelmed at being spoken to by the famous author who had the reputation of being aloof and snobbish.

"Y-y-y-yes," she stammered.

Bluntly Miss Cather put the question: "I've been wondering if I could get you and your husband to work for us at the cottage—a few hours a day, that is. There's so much that needs doing. Would you be interested?"

"Why, I—I don't know," Aggie stammered.

The baby began to fuss and she rocked the carriage. "I could talk to Ralph about it."

Miss Cather nodded. "Tell him to come see me."

Ralph Beal was not afraid of work, and he was not afraid of Willa Cather. When his wife told him of Miss Cather's proposal, he was pleased. This could be an opportunity to augment his income, and with a growing family, this would be helpful. Yes, he would go and talk to Miss Cather.

He liked the forthright, businesslike way in which Miss Cather presented her plan. They came to an agreement on the Beals' duties and pay. There was mutual respect between the two, which was promising.

45

Ralph went home and told Aggie what had been agreed upon, and although Aggie felt some trepidation about entering into her part of the bargain, she made no protest. Whatever her husband decided was best for them would surely be best. This was to prove true. It was the beginning of an eighteen-year relationship which was highly satisfactory to all parties.

One of Ralph Beal's first jobs for Willa Cather was to saw off the legs of the writing table she had had shipped from Saint John. She sat before it in a chair, showing him the proper height for her comfort. He measured the distance on one of the legs and marked it. When he returned the table, he was told it was "just right."

The table legs were only the beginning. In all ways Ralph and Aggie strove to please. Every Monday Aggie cleaned the cottage. Once she had been instructed as to what was to be done, she was left very much to herself. Sometimes Miss Cather was working in the loft above while Aggie worked in the rooms below. Sometimes she would sit outside under her favorite birch tree if the sun was hot, or in a steamer chair on the little front lawn in the sun, wrapped in a blanket, if it were cool— revising a chapter she had been working on, or reading proofs if a book were in the production stage. Miss Lewis, too, usually absented herself while the cottage was receiving its weekly cleaning. Often she walked "up town" to do errands. "Town" to Whale Cove residents was North Head, the nearest village.

When Aggie had finished her cleaning, which included changing the beds, she took the linens and other laundry with her back to her own house.

Here she washed and ironed for her ladies, even ironing the heavy sheets "so smo-o-th" with flat-irons heated on her kitchen range.

Sometimes Aggie was called on for special duties, as when Miss Cather's nieces were visiting her. Although they stayed at the Whale Cove Cottage complex, they came to Aunt Willa's cottage for afternoon tea, and sometimes for a very special Sunday night supper. These events called upon Aggie's cooking skill.

"I want to have supper for the girls this Sunday evening," Willa Cather would tell Aggie. "Will you fry chicken for us? Ah, potatoes—that way you cream them? And how about some of your buttermilk biscuits?" Then with a knowing smile, "And, Aggie, didn't you put up Lady Ashburnham pickles again? And blueberry jam?"

To such requests Aggie always agreed. Whatever it was she was asked to cook, she did in her own kitchen; then Ralph carried the hot food to the Cather cottage where it was placed in the warming oven of the range. Sometimes Aggie went with Ralph to deliver the food if there was more than he could manage.

She always smiled at how nicely the table had been set in the living room. It was a drop-leaf, which ordinarily stood with its leaves down, but for the occasions on which a meal was served in the cottage, it was moved out, the leaves put up, and a linen cloth spread. Aggie admired Miss Cather's china. And there would be flowers on the table, and candles. Sometimes there was a bottle of wine. It all seemed very elegant to Aggie.

Ralph Beal's duties varied more than Aggie's. He would plant flowers, weed flower beds, mow the lawn, trim trees and shrubbery. One constant, however, was keeping the cottage supplied with wood. This he chopped into the proper lengths for the fireplaces and kitchen range and carried in to fill the woodboxes.

One day as he brought an armload of wood into the kitchen, Willa Cather was taking something from one of the kitchen cupboards. It was a small pitcher. "Aggie likes pretty dishes, doesn't she?" she said.

"That she does. She often speaks of how pretty your table looks." He was under the impression that Miss Cather was going to hand him the pitcher to give to Aggie, but he was wrong—and a bit disappointed. It would have been nice to take a pretty pitcher back to Aggie, working in her own kitchen at home. But Miss Cather put the pitcher back in the cupboard, and Ralph went on about his chores.

That first summer, there seemed to be many "Do-you-think-you-could-make?" requests, and Ralph was glad that he was handy with tools. There were many packing boxes to be opened after items had been delivered from the Mainland, and when they had been emptied and stowed in the washroom, Ralph asked if he should break them up for kindling. Miss Cather was thoughtful, then said, "Not quite so fast, Ralph. I think we may have other uses for some of them. Do you think you could make a washstand for my bedroom out of one?"

Ralph nodded. "Likely I could." He picked out what he thought he would need and took the boxes to his workshop. When he returned, it was with a commode after the fashion of the day, with two scrolled uprights at the back and between them a rung for a towel rack. He had sandpapered the rough wood and given it a coat of varnish. "That's splendid!" Miss Cather praised. "Just what I wanted. Now do you think you could make me a chest for the bedding?"

So it went.

One day when he was working in the garden, Miss Cather came out to him. "There's a box at the store that they're holding in my name," she told him. "I want you to go up and get it when you finish there."

Ralph nodded.

Then, to his surprise, she said, "It's for Aggie."

"For Aggie?" he asked, puzzled.

"Yes. You're not to bring it here. Take it to your home and give it to Aggie."

"Just as you say, Miss Cather," he replied respectfully, "and I'm sure Aggie thanks you, whatever it is."

Miss Cather did not explain what it was. She went back into the house and Ralph went on with his work. He was curious, though. What would she be getting for Aggie, and why? He did not stop at home when he left the Cather cottage that afternoon but went directly to the general store. He was amazed when he saw the size of the box which he told the proprietor he had been asked to pick up for Miss Cather. "Heavy," he commented when he picked it up. The storekeeper nodded. "Dishes," he said.

Dishes? Ralph wondered as he plodded homeward with the package.

He lugged the heavy box into the kitchen

where Aggie was getting supper. "Smells good," he said. He set the box on the table.

"What in the world's that?" Aggie asked.

"It's something Miss Cather asked me to pick up—"

"Oh. Well, wash up now. I'm ready to dish up."

"It's for you," Ralph said.

"What?!" Aggie asked, frowning, turning from the stove.

"The package," Ralph said, pointing toward it. "Put the supper on the back of the stove and open the box, why don't you?"

Aggie laughed. "You're spoofin' me," she said. "That package ain't for me."

"'Tis too, Aggie. Miss Cather told me this afternoon to go get it from the store and bring it to you."

"Honest?" Aggie asked in awe. "What d'you s'pose is in it?"

Ralph had taken out his knife and was cutting the cord that bound the box. "Maybe I know," he said, deciding to tease her a little, since she had thought the whole thing a joke.

"It's something you got for me yourself then," Aggie said suspiciously.

"'Tis not," he answered. "It's from Miss Cather. Come on, now; open it up."

"But what's she gettin' somethin' for me for?" Aggie asked, still not touching the package.

"Because she thinks you're mighty fine help down there and do things extra. And she's right. She's showin' her appreciation. She likes you."

At last Aggie was convinced. Gingerly, she opened the box. It seemed full of shredded paper. She reached her hand in and pulled out a teacup.

"Oh! Ain't it beautiful!" she cried rapturously. She turned it around in her hand to see all the sides. "It's a scene," she said. "Oh, Ralph, ain't it just lovely?" She handed him the cup and reached in for another piece.

Ralph turned it over and read off the bottom, "'Spode. Made in England.' Sure is nice," he said.

Together they unpacked the box, Aggie becoming more awed and more excited as piece by piece was set out on the kitchen table until six place settings were disclosed. "Oh, it's too much, Ralph," she said at last. "She shouldn't adone it," but her hands were clasped in ecstasy.

"Not too much if she wanted to do it. She can afford it."

"Yes, I know, but—"

"No buts about it. Let's eat."

It was difficult for Aggie to put her thanks and her joy into words when she attempted to tell Miss Cather how much she appreciated the gift and its thoughtfulness. "You shouldn't adone it," she said again. The woman's delight, shining from her eyes, was ample thanks for Willa Cather.

The Beals helped get the gears into working order that first summer of the Cather-Lewis residency in their own cottage. In the summers ahead they would keep the gears oiled and running smoothly. This was essential in the pattern Willa Cather had drawn for her time on Grand Manan.

She wanted privacy. The Beals spread the word.

She wanted quiet. The Beals tread softly.

She wanted a minimum of matters which would draw her mind away from the story which was developing and being put on paper.

51

The Beals and Edith Lewis took care of most of the fabric of daily living in the primitive cottage. Willa Cather stitched her sampler of art. The pattern parts fit.

CHAPTER VIII

The smell of fish was strong. The taste of dulse was stronger. But the "pull" of the Island, much more subtle than these, was stronger still. Despite the inconveniences in reaching it; despite its inadequacies upon one's arrival, Grand Manan drew Willa Cather back again and again—every summer, in fact, until the war years and her own failing health conspired against their union. The mating of Willa Cather and the island was successful because the two had much in common: solitude, silence, simplicity, basics, beauty.

In the summer of 1927, when she came home to her own cottage, as close to "the good earth" as she had been in her young years, it was a homecoming of the spirit. The stars above; the earth below. She was returning to a place of her own, kin of the woods, neighbor of the sea. Now in its second summer, the cottage and its setting were beginning to meld. Outside, the front lawn sloped down to the cliff which dropped to the sea. At its perimeter were balsam and fir and juniper, but now they had been trimmed so the occupants of the cottage could see the circle of the weir immediately below, and beyond, the illimitable expanse of sea and sky. The lawn had been cut, but still the persistent wild daisies pushed through to cover the yard with bobbing white heads. Willa Cather did not mind. Indeed, she enjoyed the daisies and other wild flowers with which the Island abounded: the delicate wild iris, showing violet-to-pale-blue heads above spears of green foliage; the shining white of cloudberry massed in cumulus effects; wild azalea laden with deep magenta clusters; hawkweed, bright orange and yellow; purple clover; the demure, drooping heads of wild bluebells; grass flowers with their tiny bright blue beads strung on delicate green threads; and everywhere lupine—rainbows of pink, lavender, blue, and white.

She liked all flowers, wild or tame. So little by little, she added plantings of domestic flowers about the cottage. Rather, she planned the beds; Ralph Beal did the planting.

"A flower garden without yellow flowers is no flower garden at all," she said. Yellow had always been her favorite color. Was that because of the sunflowers which ran rampant in Nebraska in the heat of summer, followed by banks of goldenrod in the fall? Whatever it was, she had an affinity for sun colors. Edith Lewis had a yellow rose planted by the front door of the cottage. It was always "Edith's rose," but hadn't Edith chosen it because Willa loved yellow best?

Ralph Beal preferred taking orders from Willa Cather rather than from Edith Lewis and he was glad it was Miss Cather who gave most of the directions for planting and caring for the flowers. "The disposition of the two women was as different as night and day," he said. "Miss Cather was always pleasant. If she made a mistake she would admit it."

Flowers soon outlined the house, a bright rim of contrast to the grey-shingle cottage. Marigolds bloomed on the north side. On the south were hollyhocks. "Hollyhocks as high as the eaves of the house!" Beal remembered. On the southeast side of the cottage, by her bedroom door, she had him plant a Dorothy Perkins rose. As the years went by and the rose grew, a trellis was added, and the two women pricked their own hands in guiding the brambles where they wished them to go. Great clusters of the pinkish-yellow roses greeted Willa each morning when she opened the door, their delicate fragrance mingling with the dew-touched scent of pine.

In the back, a rock garden was developed; it was made of stones from the beach, and soon the purple of portulaca cascaded over it like the foam of the waves on the sand below.

Through tall, dark trees, a single-track lane cut a slash which led to the cottage. It was seldom traveled. This was the way Miss Cather wanted it. Silence reigned supreme in the woods. Only the lovely song of a bird or the "chuck-chuck" of a squirrel would occasionally break into it to make it seem the more absolute when these little wood sounds had died away.

In the cottage itself, quiet was equally pervasive. On a chilly, foggy morning, the sound of a log falling in one of the fireplaces, or the crackle of a bit of pine tossed in to feed the fire might break the silence on the main floor. Ralph Beal might come in with an arm-load of wood for the woodbox or a chunk of ice for the little wooden refrigerator; he did not drop the wood or the ice but deposited it gently, quietly. And whenever he or Aggie went in or out, one would put a thumb in the screen door to close it softly. "It was just as easy to go there and give them what they wanted as it was to bang everything," Ralph Beal said. So that was the way it was. "They wanted quiet and they had it."

In the Grand Manan cottage, Willa Cather chose to write in the loft, facing the bare rafters. Consciously, she shut out all that might distract her, visual as well as auditory. But perhaps unconsciously, she once again sought out a garret room as representing her own private world.

The attic was floored, but that was all. And as to furnishings, other than Miss Cather's sawed-off table, her chair, and her typewriter, it contained only the crude wooden chest Ralph Beal had made for storing bedding and a portable coal-oil stove for warmth on chilly days. When artificial light was necessary, it was supplied by a kerosene lamp.

This, then, was the setting. What of the life of the artist? Did it encompass anything besides her work? More than once, over the years, sometimes directly, sometimes indirectly, Miss Cather stated her philosophy that to the artist his work was his all.

To the other guests at Whale Cove Cottage where Miss Cather and Miss Lewis continued to take their meals, and to the few islanders who had brief touch with the novelist, she seemed to live scrupulously by her philosophy. She considered her writing to be art and, therefore, important; she considered herself important as a vehicle of art.

To some on the island, this seemed a fetish, a display of a super-egotist. "What did she—Willa Cather—mean to Grand Manan more than a duck who nested there for a space each summer?" a summer resident asked. "A duck of whom we knew nothing and for whom we cared less."

Perhaps this summer visitor's opinion was colored by the experience she had when introduced to Miss Cather. Miss Jacobus had made the introduction.

"My sister in New York is an acquaintance of yours," the woman said, smiling warmly. She gave her sister's name, and waited expectantly for Miss Cather's smile in return. She did not get it.

"Yes," Miss Cather responded coldly, and turned away without another word.

Subsequently the woman was to say of Willa Cather, "Like all women who have some success professionally, especially in a literary or artistic way, she had grown impossibly swell-headed."

If Miss Cather were aware of such feelings, they would not have affected her. But it is unlikely that she was aware of them, for except for an occasional excursion, she lived within the confines of her own self-appointed world, not brushing shoulders with the other residents of the island.

Though Miss Cather accompanied her friend once in a great while, Miss Lewis usually went alone on weekly trips to town for the purchase of such supplies as were needed and the transaction of business at the bank or the post office. In any event the Gilmore Brothers' taxi service was called and if Miss Cather went, life on that particular morning became a bit difficult for whichever brother drove. For one thing, she was a stickler for punctuality, and always had something to say about it if the taxi did not arrive at the exact minute for which it had been requested.

One morning when Ray was answering a call to the cottage, he was feeling quite smug for having gotten an early start. The call was for ten a.m. and, as he turned off the road onto the lane which led to the Cather cottage, he chuckled a bit. Miss Cather could hardly have anything to say this time. He was going to be there about five minutes before the appointed hour. He did not know Willa Cather as well as he thought he did.

He pulled up, turned his car around, and sat waiting. After a few minutes, the two women appeared. "Ray, you were five minutes early," Miss Cather testily announced without salutation. "I ordered, 'Ten o'clock,' and that is exactly what I meant: Ten. Not a minute before. Not a minute after."

His beaming smile broke; his good spirits were dashed. He sucked in his breath and gripped the wheel. But as the barrage continued, he reached the limit of his tolerance. "Miss Cather," he announced, "I'll take you on your errands this morning, but after this I think you'd better find somebody else to haul you."

"Oh, no, Ray!" Willa Cather protested. "I don't want anybody else. Why should I get somebody else?"

"Because we can't seem to please you," Ray replied succinctly.

"Oh, come now, Ray. I was joking. You must know I was joking," she purred. "I'm sure you know." Then, as she settled herself in the back seat, she exclaimed, "Isn't it a fine morning!"

With that the three friends bounced off down Whistle Road.

There were two annual calls the Gilmores came to expect: One was to take Miss Cather to the

Anglican tea that was given at the church each summer, and the other was to take the two women to South Head for a picnic.

One summer Willa Cather had been taken to the church as usual, had partaken of the delicious home-baked pastries, had sipped her tea, and had visited briefly with a few people there. She had done her annual social duty by the island and the church, and was ready to return home. She called for her taxi and it arrived in good time. However, its driver was neither of the Gilmore Brothers. They had both been busy when the call came from Miss Cather, and another driver had come for her.

"Why didn't Ray or Claude come?" she demanded of the driver. "They know I will only have one or the other of them drive me."

"They were busy, Ma'am."

This was no answer to Miss Cather. "You can go back and tell them I will wait until one of them comes for me and I do not choose to wait long," she said emphatically. At this point, Dr. Macaulay who, among many others, had been an audience to the scene, offered his car. "Otherwise you might have to wait awhile, Miss Cather. And Mrs. Macaulay and I were just ready to go. We will be happy to take you."

Miss Cather accepted, and the unhappy driver crawled back into his cab to the tune of Miss Cather's reproaches and her instructions as to how to register her complaints with the Gilmores.

The Macaulays were among the very few permanent island people with whom Willa Cather had any social intercourse. The doctor had been called to attend her on occasions when she had had a bout with bronchitis, which was something of a chronic problem with her. He was well read, and she found in him a ready and sympathetic mind when she wished to discuss books. This she of course enjoyed and when, on one call, he commented upon her flowers, another point of contact was made. Thus, when an invitation came from the Macaulays to dine at their home, she accepted. With this trust in the doctor and his wife established, she was willing to be transported from the tea to her cottage by them.

The call the Gilmores could expect for the purpose of taking Miss Cather and Miss Lewis to South Head at the far end of the Island always came near the end of summer and signaled that the women's departure from the Island was imminent. This clarion would sound on a sunny day when the fog had lifted and the Island was at its sparkling best. Miss Cather would be in a good mood. The summer, with its quiet and its isolation, would have been productive. The women would come out of the cottage carrying a picnic basket and a blanket. "It's a fine day, Ray (or Claude)," Willa Cather would say.

Yes, it was a fine day, Ray (or Claude) would agree.

"Not too hot and not too cold. Now in Nebraska at this time of year even the weeds are curling in the heat and everything is gray with dust—even the goldenrod."

"That so?" Ray (or Claude) would say politely.

"Yes. Only yesterday I had a letter from friends in Red Cloud. It's been over a hundred all week," and she would read parts of the letter aloud.

Ray (or Claude) would whistle. "No place like Grand Manan," Ray (or Claude) would say.

The ride from the north end of the island to the south took them through several small villages. In between villages the road at times ran close to the sea, and the sun on the water was dazzling. Interspersed with "A little faster, Claude (or Ray)," Willa Cather would observe, "Not a cloud in the sky. Not even a patch as big as your hand."

The car would begin to climb slightly, and the typical red-capped, white-coated lighthouse would come into view. Ray (or Claude) would pull up and say, "Well, here we are. You'll get a good look at the Southern Cross today."

He would open the door for the ladies and help them out with their things. "Come back for us at four," Miss Cather would say, and he would leave them.

South Head was vastly different in aspect from North Head where the boats came in. Here sharp, sheer cliffs dropped hundreds of feet to where the sea below made gusty noises as it slapped the rocks. Here there was a feeling of excitement, a breath of grandeur. And here was the Southern Cross.

After exchanging a word of greeting with the lighthouse keeper, the women would stow their gear and walk along the edge of the bank that was so high above the water that it seemed they were lonely watchers on the precipice of the world, looking down upon a gigantic chasm cut by the Creator for the basin of his mighty waters. It was an awesome spot, a site that produced a feeling of reverence even had it not been for the Cross.

But there was the Cross. Far out on the mass of rocks that jutted into the turbulent waters of the Bay of Fundy rose a giant cross, diminished by the distance, a natural rock formation, gray and rugged, truly "the old rugged Cross." As sharp as if chiseled by hand, it stood silhouetted against the blue sky, an inspiration for anyone, and for an artist surely a symbol. For Willa Cather it was a strong and integral part of The Rock she used as the basic symbol in a number of her books.

There was no sound but the breakers' crash below and a meadow lark's lyric on a fence wire nearby.

CHAPTER IX

"You remember the story, don't you, Aggie?"

Willa Cather stood in the kitchen of the cottage and watched Aggie as she rubbed black polish on the cast-iron cookstove.

Aggie wondered why Miss Cather wasn't upstairs working. But when she looked up, she saw that she had papers and pencil in hand. No doubt she was going out to sit under her favorite tree as it was one of those brilliant, sunny days that gave Grand Manan its glory.

"How Elijah 'went a day's journey into the wilderness, and came and sat down under a juniper tree'?"

Aggie nodded. As a matter of fact, Miss Cather had mentioned this story to her before. She must have heard it in Sunday School when she was a little girl, and for some reason Aggie didn't understand, it seemed to have made an impression on her. Maybe the juniper around the cottage reminded her of it.

"Elijah's life had been threatened by Jezebel, you know. He had fled to Beersheba and left his servant there and gone on into the wilderness alone." Miss Cather's voice broke off, and she stood staring out the window into the woods.

Aggie thought: "Miss Cather's a good livin' woman on a good passage." But why, she wondered, was she again telling this story of Elijah and the juniper. Why didn't she go on now about her business? Aggie had finished with the stove and wanted to get on with *her* business.

"And the angel of the Lord came to Elijah," Miss Cather was going on musingly as she continued to stare out the window. "He told him to eat and drink. And the Lord supplied him with that food and drink so he would have the strength to get to Mount Horeb." Her voice died away, and without speaking further to Aggie, she went out the back door.

Again Aggie thought: "What is it about the juniper?" Then she forgot about Miss Cather and Elijah and the juniper tree and turned her thoughts to her tasks. The little refrigerator she would do next. She would wash it out with soda water so it would smell sweet.

It was the summer of 1928. Miss Cather and Miss Lewis had come to Grand Manan this time by an even more circuitous route than usual. They had traveled via Quebec.

The preceding winter had been a particularly difficult one, leaving Willa Cather feeling both depressed and rootless. Her father, with whom she had had a very close relationship and a real bond of understanding, had died. Also, she and Miss Lewis had been forced to move from the apartment at No. 5 Bank Street, the apartment in which they had lived for fifteen years. The building was to be torn down in the name of "progress," and this in itself made Willa Cather bitter. The two women had moved to a small hotel, the Grosvenor, until they could find another apartment. They had two dreary, sunless rooms at the back of the hotel, and these too were depressing—although Miss Cather had chosen them because of the quiet she felt the location would afford.

She was eager, though, to get away from them, and the cottage at Grand Manan beckoned. But it had seemed a good idea to have a bit of vacation before going to the Island for another summer's work. Neither of the women had been to Quebec before. The trip would provide new scenery en route, and the city itself was said to have an appealing French flavor.

So they had gone to Quebec and taken rooms at the Frontenac. From the moment Miss Cather looked down from the height of the castle-like hotel onto the Norman architecture of the city, she was enamored of Quebec. She had always loved France. And here in the New World on this unlikely rock was this lovely French settlement. It pricked her imagination, and she was eager to be out, investigating its treasures.

For some days after their arrival in Quebec, Miss Lewis was ill, confined to her bed in the hotel. So Willa Cather roamed the charming, history-laden, French-Catholic streets alone. Each time she returned from such a foray, she came back with an air of suppressed excitement. Miss Lewis listened to her vibrant accounts and noted the way her eyes glowed and her voice pulsed with emotion. Something was at work here. The creative fire had been kindled again.

Death Comes for the Archbishop, written by Protestant Cather, already in the hands of the reading public, was receiving plaudits far and wide—plaudits even from the Catholic clergy—for its truthful representation of the early church in the Southwest. But its author had not begun another book, nor as far as her companion knew, had she determined upon the subject of another. Was the Catholicism in which she had been steeped during the years of work on her latest book still holding her in its grip? Was she now feeling a continuity which eased the trauma that assails an author when one book is finished and another not yet begun? Miss Lewis, always sensitive to her friend's moods, thought she could see some such pattern in process.

"The Frontenac has a splendid library," Miss Cather reported one day, bringing an armload of books into the room.

"What do you have there?" Miss Lewis asked.

"Parkman's histories of Canada. And the most interesting little volume by an Abbé Scott about this area. I dived into it a bit, and it's fascinating."

Upon her return to Grand Manan Island that summer, the memory of Quebec had filled her mind with much that was old, but new to her. So when she carried a sheaf of papers to a chosen chair in the sun or under her favorite tree, she did not always give the papers her attention. This was her wilderness, and, literally, this was her juniper tree

64

on which her eyes were fixed. The silence was absolute as it had been for Elijah. And if it was not "an angel of the Lord" that appeared to her as she sat in quiet contemplation, it was something comparable. For something, call it what you would—God, the creative force, inspiration—was leading her surely to Mount Horeb. Mount Horeb, Mount Sinai, one and the same, the mountain top where the law was given Moses. Yes, she meditated, her situation had an analogy in the story of Elijah. On *her* mountain top, inspiration had come. The plan for another book was beginning to evolve in her mind. It would be laid on "The Rock" and would continue in the Catholic vein.

When it was nearing noon, Miss Cather carried her papers inside. "Time to go to lunch," she said to Miss Lewis.

"Yes."

They set off on the path through the woods to Whale Cove Cottage.

Before lunch, came the mail. On this particular day, there was a letter from Isabelle McClung Hambourg who, with her husband, was now living in France. Miss Cather warmed at the familiar handwriting. But she did not open the letter. Edith Lewis made no comment. She understood.

It was customary for the two women to take a siesta upon their return to the cottage. Miss Lewis had slipped to her room. Now Miss Cather would read this very special letter. Her dear Isabelle, so far away, and yet so close.

The creak of the bed in the front bedroom told her that Edith was established for her nap. She took up the letter with its dear writing, and held it for a long moment before slitting the envelope.

Then she unfolded the sheets and began to read:

"My darling Willa,"

The cultivated hand was consistent, always loyal to the line, adapted comfortably to the page.

"The little piece of juniper means much to me, and I thank you for it."

How remarkable that Isabelle's letter should begin with juniper, the very subject of her own thoughts a few hours ago! Yet perhaps it was not so remarkable for she and Isabelle had always been closely attuned.
She read on:

"...When I warm it in my hand and smell it, it's all sweet pine plus the sea. By-the-sea pines are always—as to perfume— all different from the inland ones."

Yes, Willa thought, she is right; she is so very perceptive and always so close to the true and the real—whether in art or in nature.

"If you could now smell my little piece of juniper," wrote Isabelle, "you would tell Edith to make you a pine pillow for New York—It's delicious!"

What a fancy! Willa laughed to herself. Yet if Isabelle were here, she thought, this would be just such a thing as she would do—make me a pillow of juniper so that I could have a bit of the solace of silence and sea in New York. Dear, dear Isabelle.

The contents of the next paragraph were less stimulating. Yet Isabelle's concern for Willa's physical well-being touched her.

"Should you see Flo Arliss [a mutual friend, wife of the distinguished actor George] do please ask her about her doctor. Flo thinks she is going to New York. Her treatments sound like a very glorified rubbing. She has done marvels for Flo and George. I am sure she would be good for you. I would go to her if she had not left Paris..."

Then on to what she had been reading. This subject was never slighted in the letters that passed between the two of them over the years. Always they had shared their thoughts and feelings about books—about art—about music.

"I've read *The Torrents of Spring* volume. I wonder if Heaven is as good as that!
"We went to the Luxembourg Gardens this morning. The gardens were beautiful— the weather warm and full of sun—for Paris, and the sky was high and hard, not a cloud. The horse chestnuts are huge russet and green bouquets."

She is very good at description, Willa thought.

"...Just below us all the little donkeys and goats were having their lunch. Then a brushdown before the children's afternoon drives would begin. Suddenly a goat stood right up and began to chew an oleander. There were shouts of 'Philomène descend!!' Then she was tied to the iron fence..."

67

Willa, envisioning the simple scene, smiled throughout the passage.

> "In the afternoon, Nina came to tea and insisted on taking us to a spot she liked in Montmartrê. It was nice, but from one spot one was obliged to look down over the entire city—as Jan said—what hideous things cities are. When one looks at them like that, it is terrible. Paris is worse than Pittsburgh. Pittsburgh was at least colorful in a violent, ugly way, while Paris is a mess—a negative mess.
>
> "That made me think again about how deeply grateful one must be for every small beautiful thing in the world."

Every flower on this Island, Willa mused. My view. She sat looking out the front window over the Bay for sometime before continuing to read. The juniper. Every small, beautiful thing in the world.

At length she turned back to the letter:

> "Poor people. What they are obliged to undergo."

Willa knew Isabelle wrote from the pinnacle of life-long affluence. Yet Isabelle understood the shadows.

> "I began even to feel a sympathy for the Sunday crowd which I generally manage to avoid and to feel glad when I saw good, hard, tough, thick-skinned ones. There were plenty of 'em...
>
> "How ugly Sacre Coeur is when one is close to it. It is not as stupid as Saint Paul's, but perhaps even more pretentious—it is best

seen from my beloved Rue du Bac [across the Seine about two and a half miles distant] and such like."

How aware Isabelle was! How alive! How responsive to all that was good and beautiful, how disheartened by what was not! Willa read on, a paragraph about how different the large, purple figs in Paris were from the small golden ones of Florence. The golden figs of Florence! Willa saw them again, smelled them again, tasted them again—another shared experience with Isabelle.

> "Jan cleared about $1,000 on his 'cave' of old wines," the letter went on. "We were keeping them for you, but you did not come. Now the Cave is empty.
> "So lovingly to you,
> Isabelle"

Willa mused: How sad the ending! "We were keeping them for you, but you did not come." Willa could hear the reproach in Isabelle's tone, gentle, but reproach nonetheless. And her last line—that was the touch of an artist: "Now the Cave is empty." And it implied far, far more than it said.

She took the letter with her into her bedroom and put it in a small box in which she kept her few treasures on the Island. Slowly she removed her shoes and then slowly leaned back upon the bed. She closed her eyes and her visions were all of Isabelle—Isabelle in the first days in Pittsburgh, Isabelle at Cherry Valley, Isabelle in France with her, Isabelle—, Isabelle—Slowly her waking images merged into dreams of Isabelle, of juniper, of Elijah, of soft, fragrant pillows made of juniper that smelled of the sea.

69

CHAPTER X

When Willa Cather first appeared in the dining room at Whale Cove Inn with a red flannel sleeve pinned over the starched white one of her middy blouse, her fellow diners raised quizzical eyebrows. But the red banner was not to attract attention. "It's for the rheumatiz," she explained, trying to be jocular when she saw her waitress eyeing it curiously. The ills of the flesh were beginning to assail Willa Cather. It was well that on the Island there was a doctor she could trust.

Not only did she trust Dr. Macaulay as a physician, she also enjoyed and respected him as a person. There was a strict rule at the Cather cottage that no one could drive below a certain point—the end of the lane which led down from the road. This meant a little walk to the cottage. Miss Cather would have no cars turning around and making ruts on her property! When a driver was ready to leave he had to maneuver his car back and forth on the narrow road, nosing into the trees of the forest which bordered it, in order to get his vehicle turned around.

But did Dr. Macaulay abide by this "stop-at-the-end-of-the-lane" rule? Indeed not! He paid no attention to it. When he had been asked to come to the cottage to make a professional call, he drove his Model T to the very corner of the sacred structure, hopped out, banged the car door shut behind him, and, black bag in hand, reached the door in a couple of strides, called out his arrival, and let himself in. No Cather-clad rules for him: "Don't drive into my yard ... Don't slam any doors or make noise ... Knock quietly and enter only if asked to do so." Not for Dr. Macaulay! He was his own man.

"How's my favorite patient?" he would boom out.

And his favorite patient submissively, and to all appearances happily, let him break all the rules without a murmur. In fact, she welcomed him whole-heartedly, whether it was a professional or a social call that he was making.

While the Macaulay home was the only one of native Islanders' to which Willa Cather would accept an invitation, there was also a summer home to which she would go—with reservations. This was the home of two sisters who lived quite near the Cather cottage on Whale Cove Road. They were from Salem, Massachusetts, cultured, "of good stock," and one of them, at least, Miss Masters, had a good Yankee sense of humor. Miss Cather always invited them to one of the two teas which she gave annually, and she, in turn, was invited to their home at times.

There was one stipulation to her accepting these invitations—that there be no other guests. This same stipulation she had also made elsewhere. One time when she had been a guest of the Canbys, editor friends in New York, there had been one other guest, a young man. After she had successfully ruined the evening, she announced to the Canbys that any dinner of theirs which she attended henceforth would be on condition that she scan and approve their guest list.

A summer resident on Grand Manan, who was a friend of Miss Masters and her sister, when told of Cather's dictum to them, made a story of it with which she regaled guests for many years:

"Willa Cather," she said, "announced that she would not darken those doors unless a solemn promise was given her that while she was within, absolutely no one else was to be admitted. The common herd was to be notified that such was her dictum. The poor sisters used to sit in miserable dread that they might have to turn some friend from the doormat. I offered to make a gaudy sign to hang on the door knob on those glorious occasions, such as 'DANGER! MEASLES WITHIN.'"

Other cultivated summer residents had only occasional contact with the author, perhaps being invited to tea once a season. One such was Sabra Jane Briggs who had met the writer during the summer in which the Cather-Lewis cottage was being built. "I felt very definitely that she was here to work. I never went down to call unless I was asked," said Miss Briggs. And, when she dined at Whale Cove Inn, she obeyed the Jacobus order to let Miss Cather strictly alone. One time, however, Miss Briggs was late to dinner so waited on a couch in the outer, communal room for the second seating. Miss Cather, too, happened to be late, entered, and, too, sat on the couch.

She said to Miss Briggs, "I hear you have bought some land."

"Yes."

"I also hear that you bought a car with a rumble seat. I have never ridden in a rumble seat."

"Would you like to?"

"Yes, I would."

The next day they drove toward South Head, near where Miss Briggs subsequently built and managed a successful inn. Miss Briggs was in the front seat; Miss Cather, in the rumble—which caused some wag to quip that that was probably one of the few times anyone had ever been ahead of Willa Cather.

On being questioned about her association with the author, Miss Briggs thought back. "I remember once, a number of years later, I had a niece—ten or eleven years old then—visiting. We and some of my friends were out walking when we met Miss Cather coming from the opposite direction. She stopped and talked with my niece but ignored the rest of us completely. She was fond of children."

Two other summer women, Ethel Manning and Katharine Schwartz, among "the originals" at Whale Cove Inn, had casual contact with the Island's celebrity. They talked with her briefly— when Willa Cather would introduce a conversation—and once, when Miss Manning was walking by the Cather-Lewis cottage, Miss Cather invited her in and took her on a tour of the cottage. This was, indeed, a rare favor!

"I found her very simple and very cordial. I liked her very much and always did. I appreciated her wish for privacy," said Miss Manning.

Yet there was always the fear of intruding, of being misunderstood. One time after the Misses Schwartz and Manning had acquired their own house on Whistle Road, Miss Manning, sitting on the porch, saw Miss Cather going by, laden with packages from shopping. Had it been any other neighbor, without a second thought she would have volunteered to help carry the bundles. Her impulse was to call out, offering assistance. But this was not just any neighbor. This was Willa Cather. Ethel Manning stopped rocking. Should she or shouldn't she? While the tug-of-war was taking place in Miss Manning's mind, Miss Cather passed by, and, with her, the moment of crisis. Miss Manning's inner conflict ceased; with a wry smile, she continued, quietly, to rock.

Years later, Ethel manning happened to be in line behind Miss Cather in a New York tea room. That time she dared to touch lightly a shoulder of the famous novelist. Miss Cather's swift reaction was one of obvious annoyance; she bristled. But when Miss Manning murmured, "Grand Manan," Willa Cather registered first surprise, then sudden pleasure.

No matter how Miss Cather treated other Islanders, however, her relationship with the Beals remained stable and satisfying. She knew when she had a good thing, and she was careful to keep it.

"You've never eaten lobster?" Ralph Beal asked her one day in disbelief.

"No, I don't know how you manage that business of getting it out of the shell. It looks a messy job, and the lobster's a repulsive-looking creature, to my way of thinking," Miss Cather replied.

"But it's the best eating there is," Ralph Beal protested.

"I've never cared much for sea food," Miss Cather countered.

Ralph Beal did not give up easily. From time to time he mentioned lobster. Finally, one day, he said, "We would be glad to boil a lobster apiece for you and Miss Lewis and bring them down to you, ready to eat. Once you taste lobster, you'll see what you've been missing."

So Willa Cather gave in. "All right, if you insist," she said, none too graciously.

"When would you want it?" Ralph asked.

"Oh, tomorrow's as good as any. Bring them down promptly at five."

Ralph Beal well knew that "at five" meant five on the dot, and at five on the dot the next day, he brought down the two steaming lobsters Aggie had cooked, their red-gold shells shining. To him they were beautiful. But he could see Miss Cather's lip curl when he presented them.

The card table was set in the living room, salad already on and tea steeping. "If you're ready to eat," he said, "I'll put them right on for you."

Willa Cather nodded, and he slipped a lobster onto each plate. "Now if you want me to show you how to do it..."

"Just split the shell down the middle of the under side," Miss Cather commanded in the same imperative way that she directed his work in the garden, "and we'll manage."

"No, no! That's not the way to do it," Ralph Beal protested. "Let me show you. First, you twist off the claws." This he did deftly. Miss Lewis, watching, did the same with hers. "Aggie sent this nutcracker. She didn't know if you had one," he said. Pulling a nutcracker from his pocket, he neatly cracked the claws of both lobsters. Beaming, he pointed to the dish of melted butter Abbie had provided. "Now dip and taste," he directed.

He stood back and waited with an anticipatory smile while each woman tentatively took a bite of the white flesh he had opened to her.

"It *is* good," Miss Lewis said. Miss Cather made no comment.

"I'll just finish the job for you and be on my way," Ralph said. "You separate the tail piece from the body like this," he explained, arching the back until it cracked. "Then break off the flippers." This he did in an instant. "Now you take your fork and just push the piece of flesh out whole." The ladies obeyed.

He completed the operation quickly, unhinging the back from the body. "Now enjoy yourselves with the best meal you ever had," he said proudly. "When you've eaten the rest, you can suck the meat out of the small claws."

Miss Cather looked askance.

"Just suck on the end I broke off—just like sipping through a straw. The flesh is that tender."

He started to leave them.

"Come back and get these awful shells," Willa Cather called after him. "Come in half an hour. I don't want the things around," she said, nibbling daintily, still on the claw portion. Her tone was definitely one of distaste.

Ralph Beal came back in a half hour as directed, to "clear away." He noted that Miss Lewis had made good inroads into the large back portion of her lobster, but that Miss Cather had not gone beyond the claws. Stubborn, he thought to himself. Stubborn!

"I'll bet she went to the ice box and got a piece of that ham they had sent in," he said to Aggie later.

"More'n likely," Aggie agreed.

But the Beals were not offended. They, too, knew when they were well off. Miss Cather paid them regular, welcome wages during the summer months. If she preferred ham to lobster, that was her business.

However, there were times when Ralph had to swallow his annoyance, when his own experience told him surely that her "preference" was ill advised. There was, for instance, the time when she wanted him to polish the gateleg table. "Here's the Simonize," she said to him, handing him the can of wax. "I brought it from New York."

Ralph took the wax, spread it evenly over the table top, then with a large, soft cloth and the force of his strong right arm, he began to polish. Just then Miss Cather happened to be going through the room. "Oh, no!" she exclaimed. "You leave it on a while before you rub it off. Quite a while. Our maid Simonizes our furniture in New York. She leaves the wax on for an hour or more before she polishes."

"But not here, Miss Cather. I wouldn't leave it on here where you have the moisture and the salt air."

"I don't see why that should matter," Miss Cather replied. "Leave it on."

He left it on.

In a couple of hours he returned, polishing rag in hand. It was just as he had known it would be. Where the wax had stood, the wood had turned white. He called Miss Cather. He didn't say a word—just pointed to the table.

"Oh, my," Willa Cather said, adding lamely, "I guess you were right. I had no idea..."

It was during that same summer, the summer of 1931, that Ralph Beal brought a telegram to the secluded cottage. This was an ordinary occurrence. Telegrams he frequently delivered, for messages went back and forth between Miss Cather and her New York publisher via wire. Mail was slow. So he thought nothing about this particular telegram until Miss Lewis summoned him to help the two women get ready for a hasty departure from the Island. The message of this telegram had been extraordinary. Mrs. Cather had died and the distant past had caught up with the present.

CHAPTER XI

Thus another tie with Willa Cather's past was severed. With both of her parents gone, the family home in Red Cloud was sold. More than ever, the cottage on Grand Manan became her spiritual as well as physical home, and she yearned each dull gray day in New York for the season when she could return to the Island, bright with flowers and quiet with its forests.

When she and Edith Lewis arrived there the summer following her mother's death, she went willingly to work on *Shadows on the Rock*. Her writing hours were her best, for then she was lost in her story. Probings into memory, and immediate questionings were shelved. However, when the day's writing stint was done, she often sat in the deck chair in front of the cottage, a book unopened in her lap, her eyes on the far horizon where sea met sky. It was then that Edith Lewis felt the "shadows" had fallen on the Island as well as on "the rock."

More and more Willa Cather was shutting others out; less and less did she touch shoulders with the few islanders with whom she had established rapport. The agonizing problem of mortality was in her thoughts as it was in the book on which she was working. The delicate, intricate problem of personal relationships was also in both.

Edith Lewis was there, as she had been for many years. In this she was fortunate and she knew it. Willa Cather needed Edith Lewis. Edith fended off the world. She protected the artist in the woman known as "Willa Cather." Yet Willa Cather would not have been pleased at William Allen White's cogent remark that every captain must have a first mate, that "It takes two to write a book." Still, in a way, she gave Edith Lewis her due, and Edith was a part of the present.

Isabelle McClung, on the other hand, was part and parcel of her past. Isabelle was very special. But she was far away, living in France, and Willa seldom saw her. Her letters were a link with the past and a reality of the present. They meant much to her. When the mail boat came in, and there was a letter from Isabelle, her eyes, gazing to the far horizon, took on a different look. Sometimes, she even got out the letters she had previously received and read them over. They brought back the Isabelle of her youth. They were very precious.

There was the one that read:

"My darling Molly,
"Last night rather late I finished—for this time—reading 'Little Women' with a horrid feeling of having been disloyal to the great and lasting joy from one Christmas on

to others—which that book had given me. Last night and, even today, I loved and love it and its maker all over again. Dear Louisa did not make a bit of literature, as S. O. J. [Sarah Orne Jewett] surely did but—I wish in my last scribble to you I had not said 'Poor Louisa May' or some such thing, because she did such wonderful things for people like me and, of all the *Great*, I would far rather see *her* than *any* of the others except Turgenev and Chopin.

"I wish I might again have that wonderful afternoon when we went past Miss E. Emerson's drawn blinds to see *their* house—such mosquitoes! But now I wouldn't let them bite me while I *looked*. Then, I let those bugs drive me away. How foolish one can be.— Now how I long to feel each and every board of that house. I do not understand why or how, with all that foolish moralizing, L.M.A. could make her people so real. They are realer to me even now than most of the people I know are.

"Of course a part of it is because I lived on 'em during long winter months on Locust Street. Of course there were other things but those were like the stupid fly of a pigeon— going straight for their food or tree.

"The T. [Tuileries] Gardens this afternoon were warm and lovely. The goldenrod is fast drinking in all the left over summer sun. The smell of the box was strong—That always takes me straight to Willowshade and the little square bit of ground behind your great grandparents' house. That was where I first got its real smell.

"Don't misunderstand and think I object to youth being hopeful—far, far from it!

"May this rather foolish P.S. to my scribble to you not be lost like your traveling letter to me, but make your autumn fire burn just a bit brighter.

                              "A loving heart to you,
                                                  I."

Ever the idealist, Isabelle, Willa thought. That was why her friend loved Louisa May Alcott, even though she spoke of her "foolish" moralizing." And Alcott's people being "realer to me even than most of the people I know." A tiny, gnawing suspicion: Did that include her, Willa, now that the miles and the years separated them so widely?

Yet, were not the lines nostalgic that dealt with the smell of the box? And did Isabelle not today love the smell of box because of its association with Willa and their pilgrimage to Willowshade, the ancestral Cather home in Virginia? In the letters Willa felt a touch of sadness that matched her own mood. Life today was sad. Life when she and Isabelle had been young and enjoying it together was happy and exciting and full of anticipation.

She took up another of the letters. It was written from London.

"Darling Willa," it began.

Why had Isabelle chosen to call her "Willa" when she sat down to write this letter? So seldom did she address her other than by the diminutive "Molly," which she had chosen long ago, and which no one else had ever called her. But, reassuringly, later Isabelle reverted to "Molly."

"Darling Willa,

"I hope you are on your island by this time, well out of all this frightful heat—and oh, I do hope it will be lovely there all summer for you.

"Last Thursday we went to a delightful dinner party at the Arlisses in their pretty little Victorian home just half a long block from where Jan lived for years before they all went to Canada. Jenner [sic] opened the well-locked gate for us. He also served the dinner and saw to it that George was well fed. Flo says Genner (sic) is a fat lazy thing. Fay Davis (now Mrs. Gerald Lawrence—G. L. was Irving's leading man) was there. I was supposed to know who she was, remember her parts but I did not. She has been in England for years, but was born in the state of Maine, U. S. A. Was a great friend of Nordica's [American operatic star]. Knew and loved all of N.'s family. Fay Davis loves your books and knows most of them, but she had never read The Diamond Mine. Was thrilled to know about it and made a note of it at once.

"She said Nordica had her great beauty of face and her gorgeous voice but that she could *never* learn to keep time—nor to act; that Nordica's mother was the one who drove her on, obliged her to marry her first husband at the age of nineteen because he promised to pay to get N. into the Opera—finally the Jew she married taught her a bit about acting, but she was always afraid of him etc. We dine with the Arlisses again on this coming Thursday....

"Flo is a little hard on George at times, I think. She tells him rather often that it's all the train traveling she has been obliged to do

82

that has made her less strong than she would naturally be. They are two dear people anywhere and everywhere, and they are adorable in their own house. Jan made Flo accompany him a little and she loved it. I shall be so glad to tell them about the Neilsons.

"When Jan writes to Sammy, I'll add a word telling him you will be glad to see him if he goes to New York—to either write or telephone you. He will be so pleased. He sailed for Toronto via New York a week ago last Wednesday. He had a wonderful hour at the Gare Saint Lazare with Ferruccio & D. They came in to see him. Ferruccio's dream is to return to New York. He finds N.Y. just right for him. Just big enough, perhaps! Sammy always speaks of our house at V—d'Avray as the old homestead.

"Did I tell you that S. one day at tea looked lovingly at Jan's tea cup—a big one S. remembered from V. D'Avray, so I found one like it and gave it to him. He was *delighted*.

"He heard Xavier play some of Xavier's own compositions, also the double Bach with Jan and was thrilled. Sammy has the same little violin and his warm if rather coarse, heavy tone. He has learned to work, developed his taste a lot, and he has kept what he had. He has many virtues, young Sammy. Where he got 'em I do not know—in the beginning they just were, I suppose, but delicacy is not one of them and without even a touch of that—well *basta*! We were both happy to see him and he had lots to take back with him and I know he was happy about all of it. He has a voice like a fog horn, a big one—and he still has his nice dimple when he smiles. He said he *longed* to go to Florence. He has kept up his Italian *after a fashion* because there is an Italian restaurant in Toronto.

"I am writing in bed. My hand is so hot that the pen drips.

"I am sorry poor little west Virginia is a sad little thing. This is a sad time for the young who wish to work. Of course there are no jobs for any age anywhere, I know that well. What can she do, poor child! Her pictures make her rather frail and a little bit sentimental but sweet and rather pretty. Is she like that? I suppose she can't even get a job as teacher in a school.

"Oh, I hope and hope for a happy summer of good work for you my dear, darling Molly.

"I've just finished re-reading Tableau de la France. Shall I ever see the Seine again!

"So lovingly
    Isabelle"

The first paragraph and the last, Willa thought—or the next-to-last, actually. And the salutation, and the closing. Those were the biggest reasons for re-reading the letter. The chatter in between mattered comparatively little, although she was always interested in the Arlisses. But the fact that Sammy still had his dimple! Or a fog-horn voice! Or the other trivia. It was important only because it was written in Isabelle's distinctive hand. And of course because it was Isabelle talking to her.

Willa smiled at the sentence, "I suppose she can't even get a job as teacher in a school." Didn't Isabelle remember, from those years they spent together on Murray Hill, that "a job as a teacher in a school" wasn't the simplest nor the easiest job in the world? But her "no jobs for any age anywhere," ending with "I know that well" was a cogent comment on Jan's inability to secure engagements.

Why had Isabelle married Jan? Willa supposed she had wanted a home, but being with him on his concert tours, she traveled a great deal. She had evidently wanted companionship with an understanding member of the opposite sex. She had wanted to ally herself with Jan in particular because he represented the arts and the arts were her love. Jan Hambourg was not a great artist and never would be but he had other attributes, Willa admitted. He was kind to Isabelle. In return, Isabelle certainly had gifts for him—a cultural background, sensitivity, financial security, the charm of an experienced, gracious hostess—and, how well she knew, Isabelle was a giving person.

With the lapse of the long years, the acute ache of loneliness due to Isabelle's being far away had dulled. But still, when the mail came, with its routine offering of business letters and occasional letters from members of her family, the sight of Isabelle's handwriting on an envelope brought a tingle of anticipation. And to read what was inside was always a joy, a thrill.

She folded the letters to return them to their box. The day was ending. Another day would find her back at her typewriter, continuing the story of the Auclairs and Count de Frontenac and the old and new bishops in Seventeenth-Century Quebec. It would continue in its quiet, serene tone, a tone easily attained when one was living on Grand

Manan in a time when one's personal life was becoming more and more solitary, more and more introspective. After all, she had wanted to dedicate her life to her art. And she had found this spot, this lovely, quiet, isolated spot in the Bay of Fundy where one's eyes could gaze into far distances.

Yes, Isabelle, she said in silent communion, I am on "my" island, and it is lovely here. And your wish for a happy summer of good work for your Molly is being fulfilled day by day. While the Island and you are not depicted in the book, the Island is a part of the book because it is a part of me, as you are a part of the book because you are a part of me.

CHAPTER XII

So the remaining summers of the 1930's came and went. The pattern in the Cather cottage on Grand Manan changed little except that the author who set the pattern became more and more withdrawn and more and more appreciative of her hideaways. Friends who received letters from her noted how often she referred to the relief, after reaching the Island, of having no telephone jangling, no doorbell buzzing.

Lucy Gayheart literally flowed from her pen, was carefully revised via the keys of her old Oliver typewriter, went to press, was proofed and published. While Miss Cather always wrote her first drafts in longhand, working mornings, she often typed from about two to four in the afternoon, transferring a manuscript from its first to its second stage. These important steps in the book's development were all done in the attic room of the grey-shingle cottage at Whale Cove.

A book of three long short stories, *Obscure Destinies*, was brought out by her now long-time publisher, Alfred Knopf. There was a compilation of her critical essays, titled *Not Under Forty*, on which she did some editing and for which she wrote a new essay on Thomas Mann's *Joseph and His Brethren*, this at the behest of Mr. Knopf. She worked on this project through the summer of 1936. But it was then two years since she had done any work on a novel. She was having difficulty with a painful wrist, she had less physical stamina than previously and she often complained of feeling tired.

Finally, in 1938, she did begin another novel, the one which was to be titled *Sapphira and the Slave Girl*, and which was to be her last.

There were interludes between working hours, of course, during those last summers on Grand Manan. Two of her nieces, twin daughters of her brother Roscoe, came to visit during two successive summers, following their junior and senior years in college. They stayed in an adjunct to Whale Cove cottage, a dormitory-like accommodation built from an old barn. Each morning the girls, Margaret and Elizabeth, met their aunt and Edith Lewis for breakfast at Whale Cove, for lunch at noon, and for dinner at six o'clock, except for special occasions when Miss Cather served Sunday evening supper in her own cottage.

The nieces observed the rules of the House of

Cather as did everyone else. They took walks with Aunt Willa when she suggested them; had tea with her when she invited them; and stayed strictly away from her cottage when she was working.

Their walks often followed the Red Trail, as it was both easy and accessible, winding along the top of the cliffs above the cove. It was called the Red Trail because Sarah Jacobus had had it marked with red paint to make it easy for her guests to follow. There were paint marks on tree stumps and stones, but Miss Cather had no need of markers after ten summers on the Island.

To the amusement of the nieces, the walks involved a regular ritual. Aunt Willie and Edith must have their blankets for resting, talcum powder for discouraging the sun and easing discomfort if an insect should bite one, an umbrella in case of rain or too much sun, scarves to tie down hats in case of wind. By the time they were ready to depart, everyone was well loaded down with equipment. Chocolate and soda crackers also went along for snacking.

Whenever they stopped to rest, the nieces discovered that their aunt had used her imagination on the trail as elsewhere. The first stop was under a large beech tree.

"This is Wendy's House," Miss Cather said.

"Oh, Peter Pan!" exclaimed Elizabeth with a smile.

Her aunt nodded. Out came the chocolate and soda crackers.

"I'll have just chocolate," said Margaret.

"But they're so good together," her aunt insisted. "You see the saltiness of the crackers brings out the flavor of the chocolate. They work together. And," she added significantly, "it's French chocolate."

Margaret took both.

The next stop was in "The Tangly Wood."

"Tanglewood Tales?"

A nod.

Later on in the walk, Willa Cather pointed to the bluff that extended below them to the sea. "See the Giants' Graves?" she asked. Yes, they saw that the bluff had been worn by the water into large mounds.

Then they must always pay a visit to "The Grandfather," a huge spruce tree that had long ago been felled by lightning and lay on the hillside bleached white by years of sun and rain.

Occasionally the foursome went to Rose Cottage for the evening meal. There were not many places for eating out on the Island—no restaurants or cafes—only the few places that took summer guests. Rose Cottage was one of these, a spacious summer house which had been converted to commercial use. An occasional meal there offered a change from Whale Cove's fare and females. For the clientele at Rose Cottage was not limited to "the crossed in love"; during the summers of the nieces' visits, it included several couples as well as a pair of wealthy bachelors.

At Rose Cottage, Willa Cather had her favorite waitress, and the nieces knew that when they went there to eat, they would be seated at one of the tables handled by that waitress. The bachelors' table was close by, but Aunt Willie was not friendly with the gentlemen, and the nieces took their cue from her. They always noticed on those evenings out at Rose Cottage that at the end of the meal their aunt tipped the waitress well. They also soon discovered why. It was a matter of reciprocity. There were special little favors for Aunt Willie: A bouquet of fresh roses always stood on her table. The fork was placed at the right of her plate, the knife and spoon at the left, the way she liked them, because she ate left-handed. Her coffee or tea came to the table piping hot. "Her" waitress looked after Aunt Willie well, and Aunt Willie appreciated the little courtesies.

The Sunday evening suppers "at home" involved another ritual, and as with the walks, elaborate preparations. For them, the rarity of imported vintage wine, shipped from Saint John. For them, slices of ham that had been ordered from Montreal. For them, wild strawberry jam from Quebec. And for them, Aunt Willie's own salad.

The nieces watched with interest as their aunt washed each green, curly leaf of the local leaf lettuce she used, then, to dry it, tapped it gently on a towel. "So as not to bruise it," she explained.

"Why don't you use head lettuce, Aunt Willie?" asked Margaret, watching the operation for the first time.

"No Iceburg lettuce for me," her aunt replied. "It has no taste at all, and it isn't even green."

"Did you have leaf lettuce in Nebraska?" asked Elizabeth.

"Oh, my yes!" replied her aunt briskly, and the twins cast each other a knowing look. Nebraska was special. Leaf lettuce grew in Nebraska. Therefore, leaf lettuce was special!

The dressing for the salad, too, was by Willa Cather's own hand.

"The olive oil and garlic came from New

90

York," she explained as she mixed. "All of the ingredients for our little niceties have to be ordered from away. It takes some planning to get them here... You can put the bread on, girls. We had that sent from Montreal."

Already on the table was a low bowl of flowers flanked by candles.

"You may light the candles now. We're ready."

To anyone looking in on one of these occasions, the table would have seemed to belong to New York rather than to Grand Manan, to a sophisticated apartment rather than to a crude cottage. But Willa Cather liked her "little niceties," and, despite the trouble, took them with her wherever she went.

Sometimes after their Sunday evening meal, Willa would read aloud to the nieces and Edith Lewis, most often from Shakespeare. But she also had books of poetry available and some of Dickens' volumes, and she might choose to read from one of these.

On the morning of the nieces' departure from the Island, they had their instructions. "You watch," their aunt would tell them. "When the boat goes by Whale Cove, Edith and I will be where you can see us."

Sure enough, when the boat had pulled out of the harbor at North Head and had rounded the bend that brought Whale Cove into view, high on the cliff they could see two small figures waving a red flag.

"It's Aunt Willie's red bathrobe!" Margaret cried. And indeed it was.

Once in a great while during the last years

there was an Island guest at the cottage. One afternoon at tea time when Willa Cather had suggested to Edith Lewis that they have their tea outside because it was such a lovely day, they had an unexpected guest. As Willa was laying the things on the little rustic table in the front yard of the cottage, she noticed a figure on the beach below. She left her task and walked over to the bank down which a path led to the water's edge. Yes, the man she had seen was Mr. Greenlaw. She had thought so even at a distance. He had a basket, and he was gathering shells.

"Mr. Greenlaw!" she called.

He straightened, looking for the caller.

"Up here," she said. "It's Miss Cather. Won't you come up and join us for tea?"

Mr. Greenlaw was taken aback. He had met Miss Cather only once several years before when she had been on an excursion to Dark Harbor where he lived. She had had her driver stop at the Greenlaws' because she had noticed that they had a small apple orchard. But then she discovered that Mr. Greenlaw was an artist, and she had bought one of his paintings. So he supposed it would be only civil to accept her invitation to tea.

"That would be nice, Ma'am," he called, "but I'm pretty dirty."

"You can wash in the cottage," Miss Cather replied.

So that was how it came about that there were three sitting down to tea in the shade of the alders in the Cather yard that afternoon.

"And how are your apple trees doing?" Miss Cather asked.

"Oh, they're kind of scraggly. The wind's

mighty hard on 'em down there, but my wife and I like having a few apples."

"And the blossoms in spring. The orchard must be worth the care it requires just for that heavenly fragrance."

"Likely so. They're sweet smelling all right, and mighty pretty too."

Miss Cather nodded. "We had apple orchards in Nebraska," she said.

When Mr. Greenlaw said nothing to this, Miss Lewis inserted, "Miss Cather is from Nebraska."

"Oh," he said. "I see."

"My friend to whom I gave your painting likes it very much," Miss Cather said.

"Let's see. The one you bought was of the Swallowtail Lighthouse, wasn't it?"

Miss Cather nodded and lapsed into silence. From then on, as they sipped their tea and ate their little cakes, she said little. Miss Lewis kept the conversation going.

"You were gathering shells?" she asked Mr. Greenlaw.

"Yes, scallop shells. I paint little scenes on the backs of them."

"Oh, yes, I remember your shell paintings," Miss Lewis said. "You had some on sale at Rose Cottage at one time."

He nodded.

Miss Lewis wondered how he could paint. Both of his hands had been frozen during a severe winter storm years before and were now scarcely half-hands. Yet he managed and did beautiful work. Miss Lewis thought she knew why her friend had invited him to tea. He had two qualities which she admired greatly: the artist's soul and the pioneer's determination.

For nearly an hour, Miss Lewis kept the conversation going. She knew how Willa Cather's mind worked: There were two levels. The subconscious, lying below the conscious, might be doing its literary chores: mulling a word, a phrase, a thought. Then something said in the conversation going on around her would penetrate the upper level, and the door between the two would open. Momentarily, then, the two levels would become one. Shortly the trap door would close again, shutting out the conscious now. The literary musing would take over, but a new dimension would have been added by what was said, enriching the thought. So Edith Lewis minded the creative hopper which Greenlaw fed.

At last their guest rose to go.

"It was very kind of you to invite me," he said to Miss Cather.

She merely inclined her head. But her guest was not insulted. He thought he understood. She was off in another world, living with her characters in whatever story she was working on. He knew how it was. Sometimes his wife became annoyed with him when he didn't answer her. But it was really because he didn't hear her. He was in another place, lost in a vision of color and form that were to be his next picture.

Nelson Greelaw felt truly honored that Willa Cather had invited him to tea.

CHAPTER XIII

Though at the time she did not know it, the summer of 1940 was to be Willa Cather's last on the Island.

That year, when she was sixty-seven, she once again returned to Grand Manan. Physical problems had been besetting her for some time. The difficulty she had experienced with an inflamed tendon in her right wrist, each attack immobilizing her hand for weeks, had been arrested but not cured. The same condition at times also affected her left wrist. She felt secure enough leaving her doctors in New York as long as Dr. Macauley was on the Island. But then Dr. Macauley died.

One of the last things he did for Willa Cather was to attend her when a poisonous spider had bitten her on the ankle. By the time he was called to the cottage, her ankle was swollen to the proportions of a small melon, and Dr. Macauley had looked grave. He relieved her fears, however, promising that the treatment prescribed would soon reduce the swelling. "But you can't climb those stairs to the attic for a few days," he admonished. "In fact, I want you to stay off the foot entirely and keep it elevated."

Willa Cather frowned. "For how long?"

"That remains to be seen. It will depend largely on how good a patient you are," he added, wagging a finger at her as he backed toward the door.

A new doctor had been secured for the Island by the time Willa Cather arrived in the summer of 1940, but she insisted that no matter what happened to her, she would not call him. Fortunately, it was not necessary for her to have the services of a physician that summer.

Her contact with him came only through his spearheading a drive for funds to build the Island's first hospital. Willa Cather, when approached for a contribution, refused flatly. Throughout her life her contributions had been private rather than public; certainly she was not going to support a public project proposed to her by an unknown doctor.

Difficulties for the two women loomed larger and larger on Grand Manan because of World War II and because of Willa Cather's aging. There was the matter of getting messages to and from her publisher in New York. And even more difficult was the actual transport, back and forth, of manuscript or proof sheets. As the Island was in Canada, everything had to go through Customs. She always carried her current manuscript with her when she came to the Island, trusting it to no one else's hands. Usually it went back to New York the same way.

One day a large box, containing the galley proofs of the novel which was in production at Knopf's, arrived, and Ralph Beal brought it to the cottage. It was a wooden box. Willa Cather looked speculatively at it. "It's been opened," she said. "I only hope those Customs' inspectors took care. Will you take the lid off for me please, Ralph? It shouldn't be too much of a job. Look at that loose corner."

Some time later, the proofs read and corrected, she asked him to carry them to the attic. "I want room to spread them out," she explained. "They have to be initialed, you know."

Ralph didn't know, but he did as requested.

The next time he was at the cottage, it was to box them up again. "They're still upstairs," she explained. "Will you come up please?"

When they reached the head of the stairs, Ralph Beal saw that the proofs were spread out upon the floor. He stepped carefully between the long strips of slick white paper on which were printed the precious words Miss Cather had written, some of them on this very Oliver typewriter that stood on the low table.

Several times he had carried that typewriter down the steep stairs when Miss Cather had informed him it had become "balky" and had to have repairs. The first time she had asked him where to get a typewriter repaired on the Island, he had not been able to come up with an answer. "I'll have to think about it," he had said, scratching his head and looking solemn.

"We have to find somebody," Miss Cather had said firmly, "and soon, so don't be long in just thinking about it."

Actually, the best suggestion he had been able to come up with was an auto mechanic in one of the villages; he had found the man to be good with cars.

"Well, take it to him then," Miss Cather commanded.

Though the mechanic demurred, he reluctantly looked at it, found the trouble, corrected it, and sent the typewriter back to Miss Cather in usable condition. So each time thereafter that the Oliver "balked," it went back to the garage, and the mechanic always managed to repair it. The machine was getting old, and, along with its mistress, needed more and more help.

"I must be gettin' sentimental," Ralph Beal thought, noting that he felt a positive kinship with the typewriter and something like reverence for the proof sheets spread on the floor.

"I've signed them all," Miss Cather was saying to him. "The ink is dry now, so we can put them back together and pack them." She sighed. "I do hate to send them off."

Ralph Beal knelt on the floor and began picking up the proofs. "They're numbered," Miss Cather explained. "If you would just hand them to me in order—"

Not only did Ralph see that they were numbered, but he also saw the reason for Miss Cather's laying them out. The initialing she had done in India ink, and while he was not at all sure he would have recognized the sprawling black letters as "WC," nonetheless they were bold and firm; the author had not spared the ink! Each page had needed to dry separately.

As he picked up the galleys, in order, and handed them to Miss Cather, she made a neat pile of them on her lap, continuing in a worried tone to tell him of her fears about sending them off. "We've heard that Dr. Koht had some of his manuscript almost ruined when he shipped it from here to the States and it took it forever to get through," she said. "Why the Customs people can't be more careful is more than I can understand."

Dr. Koht, Ralph Beal knew, was a Norwegian who had stayed several summers at Shore Crest Lodge in North Head. He had even heard that this man, like Miss Cather, spent long hours at the typewriter. He was said to be a historian, but Ralph had not heard about his problem with

Customs. Where did Miss Cather get her information? She often surprised him with some bit of news "she had heard" about some person or some matter on the Island. "Where does she get it?" he had said to Aggie one time. "That's easy," Aggie had replied with a smile. "Miss Lewis does the shopping and goes to the bank and the post office. Miss Cather gets her information from Miss Lewis."

When the galley proofs were all back in the box, Miss Cather sighed again and said, "Now you can nail it up."

As they went back down the stairs, Ralph asked, "Do you want me to take them down to the boat in the morning?"

Miss Cather did not answer his question directly. "I just hate to ship them off like that. No telling what may happen to them," she muttered still in a worried tone.

Ralph did not reply. He secured the lid of the box, marked out Miss Cather's address, and turned the box over for her to crayon the address of her publisher on the other side. "Is that all now?" he asked respectfully, as always.

Once again Willa Cather sighed. She looked up at him. "Ralph," she said in a tone much more tentative than usual, "you wouldn't be able to take the time to—to take them over to the Mainland for me, and see them through Customs?"

Though Ralph Beal's occupation when Willa Cather had first engaged him had been that of fisherman only, he had since built up a business as an insurance salesman on the Island, so Miss Cather knew that what she was asking of him would be eating into his already well-filled time.

99

However, over the nearly twenty years of their association, Ralph Beal had become a friend. As such, he could not refuse her request. He hesitated only a second before he said, "Of course I could do that for you, Miss Cather."

Miss Cather sighed a different kind of sigh. "Oh, Ralph," she said, "you've no idea what a weight that takes off my mind!"

When Ralph told Aggie that evening about his "assignment" for the next day, he said, "It will take me all day, but I had to say, 'Yes,'; she was that worried you'd never believe it." He looked down at his feet. "I guess I'm a bit proud she'd trust them proofs to me. They're so all-fired important to her."

"Of course. I'm proud too," Aggie said.

The minute Ralph awoke the next morning he knew it was going to be one of those steamy hot days that would drench a man before it was over. But he dressed in his best and went to pick up the important box. Miss Cather was ready with explicit instructions: "It goes by Express, you know, once you get it through Customs. Don't let them open the box at all, if you can help it. But if they insist on it, don't let them go pawing through the proofs."

Ralph Beal nodded. "I will take as good care of them as you would yourself, Miss Cather."

"I believe you will, Ralph."

It was a long, arduous day, but before he caught the last boat back, he had seen the precious proofs placed on the train for New York. The box had not been opened, and, though his "good" clothes were soggy with perspiration, he was more proud of his day's work than if he had brought in a good catch of herring or sold a dozen insurance policies. He had done a good deed for Miss Cather, "a good livin' woman," as his Aggie put it.

CHAPTER XIV

Though "a good livin' woman," Willa Cather lacked the courage and physical stamina to keep returning to Grand Manan after the Second World War had introduced its disruptions to normal living. There were rumors of mines in the Bay of Fundy. And, once on the Island, one found it almost impossible to get workmen. Ralph Beal couldn't do everything required of his own household, his business, and two aging women living in frontier conditions.

While one might reluctantly trust oneself to crossing the ever-dangerous waters of the Bay with their newly added wartime hazard, what of one's precious manuscripts? Miss Cather asked. Or one's galley proofs? It was inconceivable. No, she would not return to Grand Manan until this preposterous war ended. And if the world broke in two at the end of the First World War, what might it do at the end of the Second?

So the two women decided they would visit Northeast Harbor, Maine, when they left the Island to return to New York at summer's end in 1940. Some of their New York acquaintances spent several months each summer in this Mount Desert resort. According to their report it was quiet and peaceful and lovely, not at all like its neighbor, Bar Harbor, where the weathy had built "cottages" that were actually mansions.

"If we like it there," Miss Cather said to Miss Lewis, "and if the war hasn't ended by then, we'd at least have a place to go to escape the heat." She sighed. It was difficult to think of missing a summer in her own home, but it might be necessary. Wars did unthinkable things to people; they were stupid and uncalled for. They created cultural chaos. Why the leaders of civilized nations let themselves be drawn into them was more than she could understand.

So it was that the two women with the help of Ralph and Aggie Beal sadly closed the cottage that fall and departed for Eastport, Maine. They would never return to Grand Manan. Willa Cather's love affair with the Island had lasted eighteen years.

At Eastport they took a train down the coast, got off at the station closest to Mount Desert Island, and hired a taxi for the rest of the trip. Securing a taxi was not easy for gas was rationed, but Miss Cather had always been determined, and now with money to back her determination, she was able to get what she wanted.

Unannounced and without reservations, two travel-weary women, therefore, arrived at Asticou Inn one late afternoon. Friends had reported that it was run by a man of gentle, cultured ways who was discreet in dealings with his guests. It was considered highly respectable, with a reputation for both food and service that was beyond reproach.

When the car pulled up in the tree-shaded drive, the smaller woman got out and went in. The other sat in the car and meditated. Asticou Inn, she thought, looked promising, and she did hope they could get rooms for a couple of days. She was hot and tired and would welcome any comfortable spot, but this looked to be more than that. The drive along the shore and over wooded hills had been beautiful. The village was small and lay somnolent in the late-summer sun. The homes and hostels were far apart, with wide lawns and huge old trees, so that the total landscape was of restful greens, mottled with patterns of light and shade edged with the quiet blue waters of the bay—a very different landscape from the one she had just left, yet as peaceful and appealing in its own way.

Her companion came down the steps of the Inn and gave a slight nod of her head as she approached the car. Long association often made words unnecessary between the two.

Miss Cather got out of the car. The driver began to unload their baggage, and the first period of residence at Asticou Inn, Northeast Harbor, Maine, began for Willa Cather and Edith Lewis.

Asticou Inn had nearly a half century of history behind it. In 1852, Harbor Cottage was built at the head of Northeast Harbor, one of the first buildings in the hamlet called "Asticou." This settlement, and later the Inn, was named for an Indian Chief who had come down with his band from the Penobscot area "many moons" before the white man came and established a village here.

Harbor Cottage, a handsome house with a fine view, was opened by Augustus Chase Savage for summer residents. Mr. Savage was of Scotch descent, a member of a pioneer family which settled on Mount Desert Island. He had an excellent business sense along with good taste, so he soon found it necessary to add another building to accommodate his guests. The new building was a frame structure of hotel proportions, which he named Asticou Inn. Summer guests soon filled both of the Savage accommodations—until September of 1900, when the Inn was precipitously emptied of its residents in the middle of a frightening night.

Old Ben, the family cat, sleeping by the kitchen range, wakened the cook with mad scratching and howling. His wails were the harbingers of fire. Fire in a tiny village which had no fire department! With the cook's cries added to those of the cat, all guests were aroused and escaped into the black night which was soon pierced by red-orange tongues licking and lapping at the clapboard Inn. Soon it was one great pyramid of flame. In the morning, there was nothing left of Asticou Inn but smoking ash.

Had Willa Cather known of this portion of the Inn's history, it is doubtful that she would have remained, for she was extremely afraid of fire.

The destruction of Asticou Inn I did not deter Augustus Savage. By the time summer guests began to arrive the following season, a new Inn had been built, and it was to this that Willa Cather had now come. Spacious and comfortable, shaded by ancient elms and looking over neatly tended gardens to the harbor below, it appeared almost as quiet as Whale Cove. Willa Cather found it inviting even before she had discovered the splendid library or met the Inn's present proprietor, Charles Savage.

Charles Savage was the grandson of Augustus. His father George had been co-owner and manager of the Inn for several years before the death of its founder in 1912. And when death ended the second generation proprietorship ten years later, Charles Savage had taken it on.

Charles Savage was a "gentle man" and a "gentleman." His personality was felt immediately by the two ladies who had come to look over Asticou Inn as a possible retreat and writing home for Willa Cather. The atmosphere at Asticou was one of refinement and gentility, of quiet and decorum, of charm and character. Willa Cather was pleased.

The war had not ended by the summer of '41. Willa Cather was grateful that she and Miss Lewis had found Asticou Inn the previous fall. When she returned from a visit to her brother Roscoe in California that June, there would be a haven waiting. She was sure she could reach it, that her physical needs would be well and unobtrusively cared for, and that her privacy would be treated with respect. She had completed *Sapphira and the Slave Girl* before she left for Grand Manan the previous summer, and she had embarked on no new major writing project since. Yet once she had had a visit with Roscoe, for whom she had always felt a special kinship, she intended to write again. Asticou would furnish the place. Roscoe had been seriously ill in the spring, and even though her own health was now uncertain, the journey to see him had top priority for the summer. After that, Northeast Harbor.

Besides the main building, Asticou had a number of cottages, and when Miss Cather and Miss Lewis arrived in July, it was in one of these that they were housed. This "cottage," a two-story house, was directly across the road from the Inn. It was known as Clover Cottage, and the name in itself seemed auspicious to Willa Cather. So did its location and setting, for it was well back from the road and almost hidden by big trees; and the profusion of flowers in the beds on the lawn made a mass of bright color against the green and perfumed the air delightfully.

The downstairs apartment was rented when Miss Cather and Miss Lewis arrived, as was one side of the upstairs. There were two rooms available, however, one quite large bedroom and one smaller one. Miss Cather chose the smaller for hers—a dormer room with a slanting ceiling such as had appealed to her since the days of her little dormer room in Red Cloud when she was a girl. Either she sought them out or they, her. This one made the fourth. There had been the one at Shattuck Inn in Jaffrey. There had been the one in Orchard Cottage at Whale Cove and the one in her own cottage on Grand Manan. Now she had found another and she was content.

The room was at the back of the house. It had a large bay window which looked down on the side lawn and the clover field beyond. Oh, it was the clover she had smelled! And she was sure she had heard the sweet song of a meadow lark. It was almost as if she were back in that first dormer room in Nebraska! If she closed her eyes, she could quite believe that it was so.

Thus she settled in for what was to prove the first of five summers at Asticou Inn, and the last of her retreats into silence and solitude before the final one.

CHAPTER XV

One of Willa Cather's chief pleasures at Asticou Inn was her quiet, solitary walks— solitary, that is, except for the companion at her side. The walks, like Willa Cather's life, were not aimless. Her life had direction. Her work had direction. And Charles Savage had provided direction for her walks. He had laid out trails for his guests much as Sarah Jacobus had done for hers on Grand Manan, though his were far less rugged. One of these led back of Clover Cottage. It was an easy walk, just right for one who liked exercise and contemplation but was no longer robust.

At the intersection of this trail with another, there was a little maphouse which the host had built, with seats for those guests who wished to rest. Here Miss Cather and Miss Lewis often sat to enjoy the quiet woods. The spot reminded them a little of the outdoor cathedral they had loved at Jaffrey which the hurricane had leveled. And the woods here were reminiscent of the woods of Grand Manan, to which she would not return because of World War II. Here under the arms of Maine's spreading elms and maples was her last living sanctuary.

"It was thoughtful of Mr. Savage to build this for his guests," she remarked a number of times to Miss Lewis.

Each time Miss Lewis nodded. "He is a unique innkeeper."

This time Miss Cather fingered the bench on which they were sitting, the table on which rested the hand-made map, under glass, showing the trails and the bridle paths in the area. "These pieces were made by hand," she said, "by someone with a very good sense of design. Probably Mr. Savage."

A quarter of a century later, Charles Savage still remembered: "I was intrigued that she enjoyed the pavilion. I didn't see many there. So one time I said to her when she was in the pavilion, 'I don't see many people sitting here.'

"She said, 'We like it very much.'

"I told her I was glad. 'It seems to me,' I went on, 'with all the times I've been here and seen no one, that maybe it was a waste of time.'

"'Please don't be discouraged,' she told me. 'If only one person cares, it is worth doing'."

This encounter and Miss Cather's words meant much to the Savages then and continued to mean much over the years. "Essentially they sensed Mr. Savage's frustrations and disillusioning experiences and wanted him to know that they understood and appreciated him," Mrs. Savage pointed out.

Another joy to Willa Cather, besides the walks, was the library at Asticou. It contained over four hundred volumes: fine books on Maine; leather-bound sets of the classics; many quality English novels. Mr. Savage also subscribed to the best periodicals. So Willa Cather had reading material she might almost have chosen herself.

Among the sets of books, she discovered a

complete collection of Sir Walter Scott's novels. Previously Scott had been a virtual stranger to her. "My mother and grandmother used to read him," she told Mr. Savage, "and they tried to get me to, but I never did." Now, reading him, she found that she enjoyed him greatly. When she had finished all of his books, she re-read her favorite ones.

In many ways Willa Cather came to appreciate Charles Savage. He was an artist and with an artist she always felt a special bond of kinship. But because Mr. Savage was a humble man, it was only little by little that she learned of his talents: that he played the piano, that he painted and did wood carving, that he was noted for his landscape design. She felt fortunate to have found an Inn which reflected in every aspect the gentle and artistic nature of its proprietor.

The first time she entered the dining room she was surprised and pleased to find it decorated in Japanese style. Oriental techniques of soft coloring and brush-stroke had been used to adorn the walls with Oriental scenes. Centerpieces of *bonsai* had been placed on grass-cloth tablecloths. Later she learned that the Japanese decor was Mr. Savage's idea and that he had designed and painted the wall panels himself.

When she stepped from the dining room to the veranda beyond, as she often did following the evening meal, she enjoyed the beauty of color and design in the flower beds and the flow of lawn to sea. When she began to learn of Mr. Savage's artistic nature, she could see his hand and heart here as elsewhere in and about the establishment. Asticou Inn was a lovely setting for any artist, and Willa Cather was content in finding a war-time writing retreat where wars seemed far away.

Her morning hours were spent in her little dormer room, usually with paper and pen before her. When she and Miss Lewis had first been shown their prospective accommodations, the housekeeper, Miss Ashley, had explained that the small room was the little Savage boy's in winter; the Savages used this house for their home during the months when the Inn was closed.

In later years Miss Ashley remembered: "Miss Cather smiled when I told her this. She said she thought it might improve her writing if she had a room that belonged to a child."

The first summer Willa Cather came to occupy the room, she asked to have the legs sawed off the little table which she would use for writing. It was a rickety old table, so the Savages were willing to oblige.

When the Savages were notified that Miss Cather and Miss Lewis wished the same rooms a second summer, Mrs. Savage said to the housekeeper, "We simply must find a better desk for Miss Cather. That table is a disgrace." The little table, therefore, was removed from the dormer room, and from another room a Governor Winthrop desk was proudly moved in.

Mrs. Savage herself went up with the ladies when they arrived, intending to say something about the replacement and to make some apology for the sad little table Miss Cather had been forced to use the summer before. But even before she removed her hat, Miss Cather, who had immediately noted the change, said, "What happened to my little table? I can't use *that*," pointing to the elegant desk.

Mrs. Savage quickly recouped. "Oh, I'm sure

Mr. Savage can find the old one," she said. "It was so wobbly and—"

"It will do well enough. Please have it returned right away and have this desk removed."

Before Mr. Savage returned the table, however, he put wooden cleats on the corners to strengthen it. Thus it was not ready to be returned to Miss Cather's room on her first day. When it had not arrived by dinner time, Miss Lewis inquired about it.

"Mr. Savage put cleats on the corners to steady it," she was told, "and he still has to stain them."

"I don't care about having them stained," Miss Cather said peremptorily. "I don't care how that table looks. It serves me well as it is. I just want that table back. NOW...please."

It was there when she returned from dinner.

Hence, during the last summers of her life she sat comfortably and serenely day after day before the little table in front of the window. She was not working on a novel, but on one of the long short stories which was to appear posthumously in a small volume entitled *Old Beauty*. When she had a section ready, Edith Lewis typed it. Edith Lewis also took care of Miss Cather's business correspondence so she, too, was busy mornings.

As a result, the chambermaids were not able to make up Miss Cather's and Miss Lewis's rooms at the time they did other rooms in Clover Cottage. Miss Lewis had explained that Miss Cather could not be disturbed during her working hours, and her working hours were morning hours.

The maids seemed to accept this without resentment. Their attitude stemmed at least in

111

part from the attitude of their overseer Miss Ashley who admired Miss Cather and was intent upon making her stays at Asticou as pleasant as possible.

On another matter, however, the maids were not quite so willing to please though they did what they were told. This unusual service was to hunt down spiders. After her painful experience of being bitten by a poisonous spider in her own cottage on Grand Manan, Miss Cather developed an almost manic fear of spiders. As a result, the maids were called each time any kind of spider appeared in her room. This was an interruption upon which she insisted! Sometimes this would happen several times in a season, as the woods and natural setting in which Clover Cottage was located were inviting to the species. Until it was found, killed, and its cadaver produced, Miss Cather would not return to her room. Thus with the door to the little room tight shut behind them, two girls, who were not fond of spiders themselves, would search and squeal and stalk and pounce until at last, in triumph, they would come out, gingerly carrying a dead spider. Miss Cather would then sigh with relief, thank them, and return to work.

During the summers in which Miss Cather and Miss Lewis resided at Clover Cottage, the downstairs apartment was occupied by a couple from New York. They were discreet and did not initiate conversation with Miss Cather. So she considered them compatible house-sharers and would occasionally stop to talk with them.

But the same could not be said of the upstairs tenants, two spinster sisters from Boston. They seemed never to learn that Miss Cather's reserve

112

meant that she did not care for prolonged greetings in the hall, on the stairs, or elsewhere; that she did not chit-chat. They chattered like squirrels each time they met her. Knowing that they were the Savages' oldest guests in terms of residency, Willa Cather did not complain to the management. She tried to avoid the sisters as much as possible and "to freeze" them when this was not possible. But they would not learn. They continued to talk "at her" and to "enthuse" about her return each of the four summers she and Miss Lewis shared the upstairs with them.

"Miss Cather was not rude to them," Mrs. Savage recalled, "but she did try to brush them off." This was as difficult as trying to brush off a persistent mosquito. But the sisters were almost her only irritant at Northeast Harbor.

Although there were many distinguished guests at Asticou, lawyers of note, ambassadors and statemen, Willa Cather spoke sparsely with most of them. However, there was one, Judge Learned Hand, whom she enjoyed greatly. His qualities of mind and manner were those that Willa Cather considered characteristics of a superior conversationalist.

On Saturday afternoons, Mrs. Savage always had a tea for the Asticou guests and any friends they wished to invite. Sometimes Miss Cather would "slip in," Mrs. Savage said, "for she was very cautious about meeting with groups." She liked the teas, however, because they were simply and tastefully done and because afternoon tea had always been something she enjoyed. "She always looked perfectly marvelous. Her hair was neat and by then iron grey," Mrs. Savage recalled. As to her attire: "Well, of course, I never looked into guests' baggage, but I always imagined that Miss Cather's trunks probably had far more books and papers than wardrobe. Her dress was distinctive—twenty-five to thirty years behind the fashion but with style, good, very good. Nobody could touch her."

In more ways than one, the Savages, perceptive people, felt no one could touch this author-guest of theirs. Mr. Savage soon acquired copies of all her books to add to his splendid library, and while he did not do it just to please her, Willa Cather was pleased.

At the end of summer in 1945, Willa Cather and Edith Lewis packed to leave Northeast Harbor, not knowing—as they had not known with Jaffrey and Grand Manan—that they would not return. Northeast Harbor and Asticou Inn had been good to Willa Cather. There she had found the peace and quiet, the solitude and seclusion which were dear to her. There she had done her last writing. There she had enjoyed her last Northeast summer.

CHAPTER XVI

Willa Cather died on April 24, 1947, and her remains were buried at Jaffrey, under the shadow of Mt. Monadnock. She had undergone a gall bladder operation the summer before, and so had been unable to return to Northeast Harbor in 1946. Thus, the number of years of her summer sanctums had been rounded off at thirty.

What had those summers in the Northeast—at Jaffrey, at Grand Manan, at Northeast Harbor—meant to the literary output of this Twentieth Century American author who ranks in the top of the list of United States novelists of all time? First, they had meant a mere physical release from the heat of New York City in those days before air-conditioning made apartment living bearable. This meant simply that she *could* write summers, when otherwise she could *not* have done so with any degree of comfort or success. Second, they gave her a base close to nature which seemed necessary for both her physical well-being and her mental and spiritual health, essentials to her writing. Third, they gave her the quiet, privacy, and seclusion which she felt were necessary for her work. So the three summer writing homes which she found in the Northeast were extremely important to her literary production, perhaps indispensable to its artistry.

During the years between 1915 and 1945, the years of her summer sojourns in New Hampshire, New Brunswick, and Maine, Miss Cather produced thirteen of the seventeen volumes that were published prior to her death. During this time, she also wrote the three long short stories that were brought out post humously under the title *The Old Beauty.*

My Antonia, considered by many critics to be her best novel, was the first to know the salubrious effects of the quiet, natural beauty afforded by Jaffrey, New Hampshire. The genesis of this story had come to Miss Cather in the summer of 1916, when she was spending some extended time in her old home at Red Cloud, Nebraska, due to her mother's illness. It was based on the character of a Bohemian "hired girl" she had known in her childhood days in Red Cloud. She even began writing the first chapters while she was still in the setting which would be the setting of the book.

It was this story on which Willa Cather was working the first summer she spent in Jaffrey. Again, as in *O Pioneers!*, she was using her own material, material in which she had been steeped as a child—the life of the immigrant farmers on "the Divide" in Webster County, Nebraska. This was material very close to "the good earth." In the tent in the High Mowing meadow, she was surrounded by the sights and the sounds and the scents of Nature: the wild flowers and grasses; the song of birds and the chirp of insects; the fragrance of dew-touched clover. There were no man-made intrusions: no blocking of sky by tall buildings; no discordant rasp of motors; no smells of smelters. Here in Jaffrey she was one with Nature and one with the simple life of which she was writing.

This assuredly had its effect on the natural, quiet tone of the book. Miss Cather herself was extremely pleased with how well her writing went that summer. Before she left Jaffrey in the fall, she had completed Book II of *My Antonia*.

The following summer, she was reading proofs of the book at Jaffrey, again in an idyllic setting. She and Edith Lewis often took their work to the woods using a tree stump or a fallen log for a seat. To Willa Cather reading proofs was not simply a matter of correcting typesetting errors. Miss Lewis noted that a word was often changed or a passage rewritten even at this late stage in the production of a book. These changes she thought inspired for they always resulted in startling improvement.

A number of these flashes of inspiration came to Miss Cather as the two women read the proofs of *My Antonia*. Again, Jaffrey contributed to the fineness of a fine book.

Jaffrey added a still different dimension in what it did for Miss Cather's next novel, her Pulitzer prize-winning story, *One of Ours*. Miss Cather used the World War I diary of Dr. Sweeney of Jaffrey as a substitute for first-hand information. This was a concrete instance of Jaffrey's aid to the artist.

By the time she was working on her next novel, *A Lost Lady*, she had added Grand Manan to her writing homesites. "It was at Grand Manan," said Miss Cather's official biographer, E. K. Brown, "that Willa Cather found the nearest equivalent to her stays in Red Cloud."

But her stays in Red Cloud were not periods of writing. She said she could not write in this country of her growing-up years which gave her some of her best writing material. Why did it have to be the Northeast rather than the Midwest in which she could write? She herself did not know; yet she knew that Nebraska aroused in her intense emotions. Therein, no doubt lay the key: She must have perspective. She must use this emotion "remembered in tranquility." And she found that tranquility in the Northeast.

So it must have been in the summer of 1922 on Grand Manan when she was able to lose herself in the story of a woman she had known well in Nebraska. Wrapped round by the grey fog of the

Island she was able to direct her mind's eye straight to the sunbathed prairies. The intensity of emotion she had felt there could now be remembered in this far-away place. The poignant portrait, *A Lost Lady*, resulted.

Thus with book after book, through the years of Willa Cather's gathering maturity, the Northeast played a dominant role. While she had made New York her home ever since S. S. McClure had called her there to work on his magazine, her spiritual home was in the rural districts. However, she did not choose to make her permanent home there because in New York were her publishers; in New York were the concerts and the opera which she loved; in New York was Edith Lewis's job; and in New York were friends of the years, such as Elizabeth Sergeant and newer friends such as the Menuhins. And there was habit.

Her summer-autumn retreats lengthened over the years during which she was spending time both at Grand Manan and Jaffrey, the hours and days and weeks of their spiritual refreshment becoming also habit.

A long symbolic novel, *The Professor's House*, and a short portraiture, *My Mortal Enemy*, were written during the years when Willa Cather was spending summers on Grand Manan and autumns at Jaffrey. The summers often extended well into September, for September was a gold and green month on the Island, the sunniest month of the year. In October, the glory of the autumn foliage in Jaffrey crowned Mt. Monadnock and flowed in brilliant folds down its sides and over the land at its base. October and often November, with their crisp autumn days of blue skies, were fine months for writing in Jaffrey.

In the mid years of the 1920's, she took to the Northeast her work on the finest of her later books, *Death Comes for the Archbishop*. In this novel, she had moved her scene from Nebraska to the Southwest, an area she had visited a number of times, first because her brother Roscoe was living in Arizona; later because she wished to see more of the chain of early missions that stretched like a now dingy and tarnished necklace across Arizona and New Mexico; and finally because she wished to do research about the lives of two of the priests who had been among the mission founders. This book, like the best of the Nebraska ones, had a pioneer theme and a far-from-the-city setting. And it reflected the serenity of Grand Manan and Jaffrey.

There was a brief time one summer, however, while Miss Cather was working on this book, that she tried—not very successfully—a different retreat. About seven miles from Jaffrey, Marian MacDowell, widow of the composer Edward Mac-Dowell, had founded an artists' colony as a memorial to her husband. Willa Cather had visited it and thought it a very beautiful, secluded spot. She decided to join the colony in the summer of 1926. Secluded and beautiful it was, but also, Miss Cather soon discovered it was regimented.

Each artist was furnished his own small cottage in the woods for the pursuit of his art during the day. A box luncheon was set on the doorstep at noon. Otherwise he was left strictly alone. All of this was good, from Miss Cather's point of view, except for the cold lunch at noon. She was used to writing until about noon, then having a hot meal, then a nap, then doing some typing,

119

then having tea. She did not enjoy the cold lunch nor the enforced change in her routine.

Even less did she enjoy the evening, when all residents at the Colony ate dinner together, had an evening of "togetherness," then retired to dormitories for the night—dormitories which did not have individual sleeping rooms. Miss Cather had long prized her privacy. Prior to the MacDowell experience, she had always chosen an environment that would protect it. She had thought she was doing this again. But now she found Marion MacDowell marshalling her days and trying to make her a contributing member of a group. This was not for her.

She endured it for the period for which she had enrolled, but she did *not* conform to Major Domo Marian MacDowell's rules, with the result that the summer was not as quiet and peaceful as those she spent at her regular summer retreats. The MacDowell Colony did not see her again. She went thankfully back to the Shattuck Inn for the fall months of 1927. By then, *Death Comes for the Archbishop* had been published and was receiving commendation from all directions. Much of that fall at Jaffrey its author spent writing letters rather than literature, but this too was happy and satisfying writing, for the letters were in response to ones praising the book.

Shadows on the Rock was to be Miss Cather's next novel, the one for which the idea had been born in Quebec the summer she and Miss Lewis had gone there enroute to Grand Manan. Much of the book was written on the Island during the summer of 1928. It was a particular joy to be able to write in the rough, beamed attic that summer, the silence unbroken save for the sounds of Nature. The comfort she knew with the Beals taking care of her physical needs; the peace she knew with the forest closing in behind her, the sea stretching out before her—were echoed in the quiet tone of the story which she was writing, a story of Old Quebec in the days of Count Frontenac.

The exquisite beauty and serenity of tone which marked the book with excellence were surely enhanced by the environment in which they were written.

Two novels remained, in Miss Cather's literary output, plus a number of shorter stories. Through both novels, *Lucy Gayheart*, published in 1935 and *Sapphira and the Slave Girl* in 1940, she continued to work at Grand Manan. Her rendezvous with Nature at Jaffrey, however, was not repeated after 1937, due to the horrible destruction in the summer of '38 of the trees which had formed her outdoor cathedral. When the havoc wrecked by the severe hurricane was reported to her by her friends, the twisted, ragged wreckage described, she had no desire to return. Nor did she return, except for burial.

The meaningfulness of the Northeast, however, had flowed as life blood into her writing during those years before the hurricane cut her off from Jaffrey and the Second World War, from Grand Manan.

And there were yet good years when the refuge of Northeast Harbor fed her creativity and helped her to produce the satisfying stories which comprised the posthumous volume, *The Old Beauty*.

CHAPTER XVII

"That kitchen with the shining windows was dear to him; but the sleeping fields and bright stars and the noble darkness were dearer still," Willa Cather had the title character say in the story "Neighbour Rosicky." Later in his musings came the passage: "In the country, if you had a mean neighbour, you could keep off his land and make him keep off yours. But in the city, all the foulness and misery and brutality of your neighbours was part of your life." And still later, "It seemed to Rosicky that for good, honest boys like his, the worst they could do on the farm was better than they would be likely to do in the city."

To Willa Cather herself the sleeping fields and bright stars and the noble darkness that she found in rural areas were "dearer still." Her character's thoughts on privacy expressed her own philosophy. His conclusion that the worst one could do with one's life and work in the country was likely better than what one could do with it in the city was hers.

In many instances in Willa Cather's short stories, her own feelings for and about the country were expressed through the words and thoughts of her characters. For her, during most of her writing life, the country was Jaffrey, Grand Manan and Northeast Harbor.

The volume of stories in which "Neighbour Rosicky" appeared was titled *Obscure Destinies*. It was published by Knopf in 1930 and contained two other stories: "Old Mrs. Harris" and "Two Friends." All three of the stories drew on the country and characters of Miss Cather's childhood for their material. They were rural stories of rural people and, in the words of E. K. Brown, they were "rich in affection for the characters and for the life she depicted." Remembered in the tranquility of the country she had adopted because it did so much for her and her writing.

The title "Obscure Destinies," one of her simplest and most effective, also speaks eloquently of her respect for the land and the people in obscure places—places such as those she sought out in which to write.

Her last writing, two stories for the compilation *Old Beauty*, was done largely at Northeast Harbor. There, in Clover Cottage, with the hum of bees and the strong, spicy scent of clover coming to her through the open window, she wrote "The Best Years," laid in rural Nebraska in the time of the best years of Willa Cather's own life; and "Before Breakfast," surprisingly a story set on Grand Manan Island, the home of her writing maturity.

She always said she would not write about Jaffrey or Grand Manan because she "did not want them spoiled." Now, however, when Grand Manan was denied her, she wrote about it, as time and again she had gone back to writing about Nebraska after she had left it. It was never events and places of the moment about which she wrote. For Willa Cather it was always the past, and now Grand Manan lay in her past.

In the story "Before Breakfast," she described in some detail her own cottage, using it as the hideaway of her protagonist Henry Grenfell, a business tycoon who had "discovered" an island, clearly Grand Manan, where he went to escape both business and family. (Willa Cather had also used it to get away from business and, though not family, from people.) "The cabin modestly squatted on a tiny clearing between a tall spruce wood and the sea, sat about fifty yards back from the edge of the red sandstone cliff which dropped some two hundred feet to a narrow beach."

She referred to the kitchen in the cabin as the "little dining-car kitchen," an apt description of her own.

All through the story, through Grenfell, she expressed her own feeling of belonging and the joy of returning to the cottage each summer. Grenfell had opened a closet door and found his old bathrobe where he had left it "two summers ago. That was a satisfaction....It made this cabin seem more his own to find things, year after year, just as he had left them."

She also described the island: the glory of its views, the challenge and reward of its trails. "The east was already lightening; a deep red streak burst over the sky-line water, and the water itself was thick and dark, indigo blue—occasionally a silver streak, where the tide was going out very quietly." A little farther on she wrote, "The sun leaped out of the sea—the planet vanished." Speaking of the island's having once been "a naked rock," she said: "Almost anywhere on the open downs you could cut with a spade through the dry turf and roll it back from the rock as you roll a rug back from the floor." She knew her island well.

And she loved it: "The spruces stood tall and still as ever in the morning air; the same dazzling spears of sunlight shot through their darkness. The path underneath had the dampness, the magical softness which his feet remembered. On either side of the trail yellow toadstools and white mushrooms lifted the heavy thatch of brown spruce needles and made little damp tents." This was Willa Cather writing about the trail Willa Cather had walked, with Willa Cather's feeling for it evidenced in every word. If there had been no Grand Manan retreat for her, there would have been no "Before Breakfast."

Even more telling was what she said of the relationship between man and Nature. On Grenfell's return to the island, he thought gratefully, "Nothing has changed." Everything was the same and he was the same. "The relationship was unchanged." It was just such an unchanging relationship between Willa Cather and the Northeast that gave her not only the material for this story, but also the feeling that went into the quiet tone and tranquil atmosphere and uncluttered settings of most of her writing.

When Grenfell had reached the top of the cliff to which the Red Trail led, he thought, "A splendid sight ... and all his own. Not even a gull—they had gone screaming down the coast toward the herring weirs when he first left the cabin."

Then came the line which gave the secret of Willa Cather's close tie with her three summer homes: "People are really themselves only when they believe they are absolutely alone and unobserved." She had to be "absolutely alone," as she could be in these three sanctuaries, before she could be herself. And only when she was wholly herself could she be the artist able to produce literature of the highest order. "In a low cabin on a high red cliff overhanging the sea, everything that was shut up in him, under lock and bolt and pressure, simply broke jail, spread out into the spaciousness of the night, undraped, unashamed."

Grenfell "had left his burden at the bottom of the hill." So too must Willa Cather have left her burdens when she retreated to Grand Manan, or Jaffrey, or Northeast Harbor.

"Before Breakfast" was not as good a story as "The Best Years," but it disclosed her relationship to the Northeast as sharply as a line drawing. When all this that was "shut up" in Willa Cather "broke jail" in the Northeast, it may have "spread out into the night," but in the morning it was gathered in to fill the pages of manuscript.

"The Best Years" must have been a joy to Willa Cather to write, for it dealt with the years of her childhood in Nebraska. An additional pleasure was the fact that it was written for her brother Roscoe, the prototype for the heroine's brother in the story.

This is the only piece of writing in which Willa Cather mentions Maine. The reference is in the last sentence: "Mrs. Thorndike did not see her old friend again, but she wrote her a long letter from Wiscasset, Maine..."

However, the effect of Maine, of the quiet, close-to-Nature atmosphere of Northeast Harbor, is in every line of the story. It was set in "the beautiful Nebraska land which lies between the Platte River and the Kansas line." And the County Superintendent of Schools, Miss Evangeline Knightly—who might well have been Mrs. Eva J. Case of Willa's Red Cloud days—"drove slowly" through it, "for she loved the country," even as Miss Cather loved it. "Between her and the horizon the white wheels of windmills told her where the farmhouses sat." Willa Cather was remembering. In the tree-shaded harbor where she wrote, she could relive the time of the treeless plains, for the quietude was the same, the insect sounds and the earth smells were the same. There were even the sloping sides of the dormer room in which she wrote, like those of the dormer room *about* which she wrote. For in the Ferguesson family of her story, as in the Cather family, there were four boys whom their sister adored and who, with her, slept in the attic, which to all of them was the finest place in the world.

The sister, "little Lesley," liked her name pronounced softly, with a "z" sound for the "s." This "made it seem gentler..." Even so, did Willa Cather want the name "Cather" pronounced with a dot over the "a," for to her ear the sound was softer and more harmonious than a short "a."

This gentle story reflected the harmony which Miss Cather felt at Asticou Inn in Northeast Harbor. So it was with the Ferguesson family in "The Best Years." And after fortune had smiled and they had built a big house "up town," Mrs. Ferguesson says of her boys, "I know at the bottom of their hearts they wish they was back in the old house...sleeping in the attic."

There is much of nostalgia in this last story, but it is not sentimental. Miss Cather is looking back across the vast stretches of country which lay between her present abode and that of her childhood. She is looking back from the promontory of success to the flat lands of her unfulfilled years and finding those flat lands and those early years "the best years." She has Mrs. Ferguesson say, "Well, this I know: our best years are when we're working hardest and going right ahead when we can hardly see our way out." Though she had long since reached a position of affluence, there had been those years for Willa Cather too. In retrospect she recognized them as her best.

Although there were times when some people did not think her so, Willa Cather was human. "The Best Years" was written with love to one whom she loved. She anticipated her brother's pleasure in reading it. With these thoughts she prepared the manuscript for mailing to him. But then came the telegram announcing his death. Willa Cather suffered numbness, then heartache—just like anyone else.

Throughout the years she had submitted to no living person. She had submitted only to her subject, and her subject was in such close union with landscape that often the two were one. Now, nearing the end of her life, with confidence she sat at her little sawed-off table in her quiet dormer room in the quiet of Northeast Harbor and wrote this quiet story, the final fruition of her literary years. In her story and in her life, the person fit the place and the place, the person.

Always place had meant much to her. She had loved and drawn succor from the plains of the Midwest, from the massive strength of Mt. Monadnock in New Hampshire, and from the forest, the cliffs, and the sea at Grand Manan Island in the Bay of Fundy. Now for her last literary efforts, she was drawing her strength from Northeast Harbor, Maine.

Perhaps she loved places more than she loved people. At least these certain few places were of paramount importance in her life and to her art. The people whom she portrayed best were always the people whose place was close to Nature.

CHAPTER XVIII

Though all three of Willa Cather's sanctuaries in the Northeast still exist today, they do not exist as she knew them. The encroachments of the years have brought change.

For a time it seemed that her cottage on Grand Manan was no longer to exist at all. It was allowed to fall into decay and was ravished.

When Willa Cather and Edith Lewis left the Island for what proved to be the last time, they told the Beals, as they had done upon every other leave-taking since the cottage was built: "Now if you see anything to be done around the place, see to it that it's done."

Ralph Beal knew there were things that needed to be done at that very moment, but he said nothing. The work most urgently needed—reflooring—was due to the mistake Miss Cather had made long ago in choosing the location on which the cottage was to be built.

"She had it built close to the ground, in this hole he explained years later, "and so the water ran down and stood at the back and rotted the wood." So the ell which housed Willa Cather's bedroom had been reflooded earlier. Now other floors badly needed to be replaced.

"They knew and I knew and anyone who was ever in the cottage knew the kitchen floor was gone and Miss Lewis's bedroom floor was gone. It wasn't safe to walk on."

"If you see anything to be done around the place, see to it that it's done." Ralph Beal remembered, but during the war years, it was next to impossible to find labor, and it would be hazardous to attempt to get materials from the Mainland for reflooring the cottage. So time went by, and the floors rotted out, and the women did not return. Something must be done, the Beals decided, for now rats and small woods animals would be able to get into the cottage. All of Miss Cather's things were there, and they must be protected.

Then came news of Willa Cather's death, and somehow it seemed to Ralph Beal more urgent than ever that the cottage and the novelist's belongings which it housed should be saved. His sense of immediacy was abetted by the fact that the war was over and he would now be able to get material.

Thus in the spirit of what he thought to be the wishes of its one-time residents, he sent to the Mainland for lumber to replace the two rotted floors in the cottage. He sent the bill for it to Edith Lewis, with a covering letter.

But Ralph Beal had made a mistake. Edith Lewis was much disturbed about what he had done. She wanted no repairs made on the cottage. The lumber was to be returned.

Ralph Beal found someone on the Island who could use the lumber, sold it to him for cash, and so paid the lumber bill.

The cottage, once proud, though humble, continued to deteriorate, and part of the roof fell in. Ralph Beal reported to Edith Lewis.

She replied that nothing was to be done to the cottage, nor to the grounds.

The grass grew. The juniper curtained the ocean view. The flowers reseeded themselves. Some died or, like Edith Lewis's rose, reverted to the wild state from which they had been bred.

130

Ralph Beal mused, "So I made up my mind that Miss Lewis wanted the place to die with Miss Cather."

After Miss Cather's death, Miss Lewis thought her reason for returning to the Island was gone. She never returned.

The Beals continued to receive Christmas cards and warm letters from Edith Lewis, though they were no longer paid employees. In the same friendly way, they continued to do what they could to maintain the interior of the shuttered cottage. On one of their calls, they found that it had been broken into. They immediately contacted the police and again wrote Miss Lewis. Again she refused to have anything done. The Beals nailed the cottage up. Yet in a few days they would find the windows open again, and would again contact the police.

Finally the condition of the cottage became so bad that Mrs. Beal wrote: "It wouldn't take a very big snow storm for it to go. Everything would fall in!" This was in 1960, and she received the following reply from Edith Lewis: "I should have told you fifteen years ago to have taken the silverware and the chinaware and any furniture you could use out of there... I want you to have all the rugs and any of the furniture you can use and all the silverware..."

"But the rugs were all mildewed," Mrs. Beal said. "There wasn't any silverware left. And as for the chinaware, there wasn't any chinaware..."

Dora McLaughlin, born and brought up on Grand Manan, but only a child at the time of Miss Cather's final leave-taking from the Island, returned home from time to time after she had gone away to college and later, when she had become a

131

psychiatric nurse. Each time she returned, she found herself following the woodland path to the Whale Cove Cottage that had been the summer retreat of the famous novelist about whom she had heard many Island tales and in whom she had become particularly interested while studying American Literature.

"I had been told that it had been left just the way it was when Miss Cather and Miss Lewis left it that last summer. Clothes were even hanging in the closets. Bedding stored in chests. Dishes in the cupboards and that sort of thing...Neither ever came back. They just simply *left* it."

Then one summer when Dora McLaughlin returned, she found the place ransacked. Rugs, dishes, furniture were strewn about the yard. Willa Cather's typewriter, lying against a log, had been demolished. There were papers all over—letters and parts of manuscripts matted in the grass and shrubbery, everything wet.

The door was off by then, and she went in. There were still things about that the vandals hadn't wanted—quite a number of hats, all with Saks-Fifth-Avenue labels. They were colorful and extremely feminine in contrast to most of the clothes, which were mannish and utilitarian: tweeds, high-laced boots.

In the loft, amazingly, there stood Willa Cather's little writing table, still intact.

"It was all so sad."

The writing table has since been given to the Island Museum, and stands in the entrance hall. But not even a Chicago typewriter expert could restore the rusted and shattered Oliver on which the novelist had composed some of her best novels.

There came a time when well-meaning Islanders wished to take over the cottage, "to fix it up, have writers work there—something like the MacDowell Colony in New Hampshire." Had this become reality, it would have been ironic in the light of Miss Cather's feeling about the MacDowell Colony.

But Edith Lewis nipped this plan in the bud. When queried, she replied kindly but firmly that Willa Cather had wanted her books to be her only memorial.

Yet the cottage was not to be allowed to die with Willa Cather, as Ralph Beal had feared and as perhaps Miss Lewis desired. Though for almost a quarter of a century it seemed to be dying the long, slow, sad death of neglect, it was rescued just short of its demise. A member of Miss Cather's own family, Helen Cather Southwick, daughter of Willa's brother James, saved it from the last ravages of time, weather, and inattention. She had never visited her aunt on Grand Manan but had heard much about the Island and the cottage. Now living with her family in Pittsburgh, Mrs. Southwick began thinking about the possibility of securing Willa Cather's cottage for a summer home. The Island was not too far distant for her family to reach for vacation periods. And it did seem a pity that her aunt's cottage should be taken over by the wilderness.

In the mid '60's, she began negotiations with Edith Lewis in New York in an attempt to purchase the property. Her first responses were not encouraging. Edith Lewis was ill and seemed not to wish to be bothered with business. She apparently had long since consigned the Grand Manan property to the forest.

Helen Southwick persisted. She and her husband made a trip to the Island, ascertained the condition of the cottage, and found the lot lines. Finally, in the summer of 1967, just twenty years after Willa Cather's death, having exhibited a tenacity reminiscent of her aunt, she filed in the Charlotte County Registry Office in Saint Andrews, New Brunswick, a deed to two lots, No's 25114 and 26509. The deed read "Edith Lewis to Helen C. Southwick."

Then began the painstaking work of removing the underbrush that had completely overgrown the yard and drive and all but swallowed the cottage; then of renovating the decrepit cottage and making the improvements necessary for present-day living.

The bulldozers and the carpentry crew went to work.

Again there was a clearing in the forest.

A new roof, new windows, new floors.

A bathroom where there had previously been only a washroom.

A modern kitchen with an electric range in place of the wood-burning cookstove; an electric refrigerator instead of the little wooden ice-box; new kitchen cabinets.

Electric lights where there had been kerosene lamps.

A telephone where there had been none.

But the floor plan of the cottage remains basically unchanged. The grey-shingled exterior is the same. The view of the cove below with its filigree of weirs is as Willa Cather saw it. On sunless days, the fog still wraps the little grey cottage in a great grey blanket. On sunny days, the world still sparkles.

134

It is not as it was for Willa Cather. Yet it is as it was for her. And in the way that matters most, it is unchanged: in its quietude, its tranquility, its closeness to the land.

Nor is the Shattuck Inn at Jaffrey as it was for Willa Cather. Instead of bearing the name "Shattuck Inn," it has become "The Queen of Peace Seminary." Instead of summer guests, it has year-round students preparing for the priesthood and august Fathers who train them. A stone chapel has been added at the north side of the Inn. But the basic, sprawling, ungainly wooden structure still stands as of old. Even the little garret room which was Willa Cather's remains the same. The glory of autumn foliage is still breathtaking. The massiveness of Mt. Monadnock still broods over all.

Shattuck Inn is not as it was for Willa Cather. Yet in the way that matters most, it is unchanged: in its silence, in its peacefulness, and in its proximity to Nature.

Asticou Inn at Northeast Harbor is not as it was for Willa Cather. It is not the same in clientele. Not the same in management. More commercial in its atmosphere. But the stately building is the same, and the huge elms which shade it. The graceful staircase. The wide verandah with its view over the multi-colored flower gardens to the harbor below.

Yet in the way that matters most, it is unchanged: in its seclusion, in its serenity, in its rural atmosphere. These continue to permeate the writing havens of Willa Cather.

But what is more important, their quiet and

serenity permeate the very timbre of Willa Cather's writing, where no change great or small can touch them; where they will always be.